Physical Security for IT

Related Titles from Digital Press

Computer Security and Computer Forensic Related Book Titles:

Casey, *Handbook of Computer Crime Investigation*, ISBN 0-12-163103-6, 448pp, 2002.

Kovacich, *The Information Systems Security Officer's Guide*,
ISBN 0-7506-7656-6, 361pp, 2003.

Boyce & Jennings, *Information Assurance*, ISBN 0-7506-7327-3, 261pp, 2002.

Stefanek, *Information Security Best Practices: 205 Basic Rules*,
ISBN 0-878707-96-5, 194pp, 2002.

De Clercq, *Windows Server 2003 Security Infrastructures: Core Security Features*,
ISBN 1-55558-283-4, 752pp, 2004.

Rittinghouse, *Wireless Operational Security*, ISBN 1-55558-317-2, 496pp, 2004.

Rittinghouse & Hancock, *Cybersecurity Operations Handbook*,
ISBN 1-55558-306-7, 1336pp, 2003.

Ransome & Rittinghouse, *VoIP Security*, ISBN 1-55558-332-6,
450pp, 2005.

Speed & Ellis, *Internet Security*, ISBN 1-55558-298-2, 398pp, 2003.

Erbschloe, *Implementing Homeland Security for Enterprise IT*,
ISBN 1-55558-312-1, 320pp, 2003.

Erbschloe, *Physical Security for IT*, ISBN 1-55558-327-X,
320pp, 2005.

XYPRO, *HP NonStop Server Security*, ISBN 1-55558-314-8, 618pp, 2003.

For more information, visit us on the Web at http://books.elsevier.com/.

Computer Security and Computer Forensic Related Products:

Newsletters and Journals from Elsevier:

Digital Investigation – New in 2004
Edited by Eoghan Casey, this new peer reviewed journal focuses on best practice, new
developments and proven methodologies in the field of digital forensic science. For further
information, please visit: http://www.compseconline.com/digitalinvestigation/

- Biometric Technology Today
- Card Technology Today
- Computer Fraud & Security
- Computer Law and Security Report
- Computers & Security
- Information Security Technical Report
- Network Security
- Infosecurity Today

For more information, visit us on the Web at http://www.compseconline.com/.

Physical Security for IT

Michael Erbschloe

ELSEVIER
DIGITAL
PRESS

Amsterdam • Boston • Heidelberg • London • New York • Oxford
Paris • San Diego • San Francisco • Singapore • Sydney • Tokyo

Elsevier Digital Press
30 Corporate Drive, Suite 400, Burlington, MA 01803, USA
525 B Street, Suite 1900, San Diego, California 92101-4495, USA
84 Theobald's Road, London WC1X 8RR, UK

⊗ **This book is printed on acid-free paper.**

Library of Congress Cataloging-in-Publication Data
Application submitted

British Library Cataloguing in Publication Data
A catalogue record for this book is available from the British Library

ISBN: 1-55558-327X

For all information on all Digital Press publications
visit our Web site at www.digitalpress.com

Printed in the United States of America
04 05 06 07 08 09 9 8 7 6 5 4 3 2 1

To my mother
To my friends in Alexandria,
Virginia, who made my stay there interesting.

Contents

Preface

The physical security of IT, network, and telecom assets is as important as cyber security. We justifiably fear the hacker, the virus writer, and the cyber terrorist. But the disgruntled employee, the thief, the vandal, the corporate foe, and yes, the terrorist can easily cripple an organization by doing physical damage to IT assets. In many cases such damage can be far more difficult to recover from than a hack attack or malicious code incident.

It does little good to have great computer security if wiring closets are easily accessible or individuals can readily walk into an office and sit down at a computer and gain access to systems and applications. Even though the skill level required to hack systems and write viruses is becoming widespread, the skill required to wield an ax, hammer, or fire hose and do thousands of dollars in damage is even more widely held.

Although many books cover computer security from one perspective or another, they do not thoroughly address physical security. This book shows organizations how to design and implement physical security plans. It provides practical, easy to understand and readily usable advice to help organizations improve physical security for IT, network, and telecom assets.

Michael Erbschloe
Alexandria, Virginia

Acknowledgements

I would like to acknowledge all of the staff at Butterworth-Heinemann who worked hard to make this book possible. I appreciate all of their efforts.

My friends and companions, Brandon L. Harris and Tonya Heartfield gave great advice and feedback on the concepts and content of this book. As always, I acknowledge the ongoing support and friendship of John Vacca. I also acknowledge the work of my editorial assistant Kayla Lesser who helped to keep the work focused.

Michael Erbschloe

Introduction

The obsession about cyber security has far too often overshadowed the need for improving physical security of IT, network, and telecom assets. During the last decade a great deal of attention has been focused on the cyber aspects of information systems security. The growth of distributed computing combined with the widespread use of off-the-shelf software products and Internet connectivity has created security nightmares for many organizations. In an effort to address an array of cyber security problems many organizations have hired or trained new IT security personnel and dramatically increased spending on computer security products. It appears that the struggle to improve cyber security will continue well into the future.

However, it does little good to have great cyber security if people can easily walk into an office and sit down at a computer and gain access to systems and applications. Likewise, it takes little skill for an individual to use an ax, hammer, or fire hose to damage or destroy electronic equipment. Damage resulting from such incidents can be far more difficult to recover from than a hack attack or malicious code incident and can cost more money.

This book shows organizations how to design and implement security plans to prevent the physical destruction of, or tampering with computers, network equipment, and telecommunications systems.

Chapter 1 provides an overview of physical security and the many reasons it is so important. These include guarding against damage done by disgruntled employees and angry former employees who have or can get access to facilities and equipment to inflict damage. There are also numerous other threats for which protection is useful, including activists and corporate foes, random vandals, industrial saboteurs, thieves, spies, and even terrorists.

The process of establishing a physical IT security function in an organization is covered in Chapter 2. Topics include where in an organization the physical security function should be established, along with how to staff the physical IT security effort. There are also several interdepartmental relationships that are helpful in developing and maintaining a physical security program. In most cases corporate security, IT security, and network security personnel can contribute to physical security planning and management. External relationships are also important, including relationships with law enforcement and private security providers.

The steps to developing a physical security plan are presented in Chapter 3. This includes an overview of the planning process and methods for plan development. Integrating the physical IT security plan with other security plans is an important part of the planning process. The integration approach also can save time and money by utilizing risk exposure analyses that have been performed. The physical security plan should be integrated with:

- Cyber security planning
- Disaster recovery planning
- Business continuity planning
- Organization risk management and insurance planning
- Incident response team planning and development

Chapter 4 explains the major elements of a physical IT security plan, including the overview and mission statement, assignment of organizational responsibilities, the use of duty officers, and the management of contact lists. The chapter also covers security procedures for:

- Data centers
- Wiring and cabling
- Remote computers
- Desktops
- Department-based servers
- Telecom and data communications equipment
- Manufacturing control equipment
- Surveillance and alarm systems

Chapter 5 provides a detailed discussion on how to develop and document methods and procedures for the planning areas covered in Chapter 4. This includes some best practices and recommendations provided by government agencies and industry associations that have been developed to address potential terrorist threats.

It is important to have good auditing and testing procedures in place to assure that methods and procedures do actually work. Chapter 6 covers the importance of testing and how to test and audit procedures. This includes details in auditing and testing methods and procedures for the planning areas covered in Chapter 4.

The steps for managing response to an incident are covered Chapter 7. This includes the initial steps of a receipt of a first report, confirmation of the incident, and mobilization of the response team. Each of the steps necessary to resolve the incident after confirmation is also covered, including notifying appropriate managers, using alert systems, informing personnel that may be affected by the incident, preserving evidence, and calling in law enforcement.

Education, training, and awareness are all necessary to the successful implementation of any information security program. These three elements are related but are distinctly different in what they require to be successfully accomplished. A model training program for physical IT security is presented in Chapter 8. This includes training for IT professionals and how to provide basic information physical security for IT assets. Training modules for non-security employees are also provided, including how to identify potential threats, what to do if there is suspicious behavior, what to expect from the incident response team, how the internal alert system works, and what employees should do if the organization is on alert.

Chapter 9 takes a look at the future of physical security for IT assets. This includes how national security plans may affect the security needs of individual organizations and the role of Information Sharing and Analysis Centers (ISACs). National efforts to improve the capabilities of law enforcement and national and global intelligence efforts are also examined.

Appendix A provides a compendium of physical security resources and Appendix B provides a glossary and list of acronyms. Appendix C is a compilation of all of the action items for improving physical IT security from the chapters in the book. Appendix D is a compilation of all of the checklists and sample forms from all of the chapters in the book.

Physical Security Overview

Physical security for IT equipment, network technology, and telecommunications assets has been drastically overlooked in many organizations during the last decade. This was caused in part by large numbers of organizations installing additional computer equipment, local area networks (LANs), and gateways to wide area networks (WANs) in buildings that did not have facilities that were specifically designed facilities to accommodate the equipment.

This chapter provides an overview on why physical security is important and how a physical security program relates to a cyber security program. In addition, basic steps on how to guard against physical attacks executed by disgruntled employees, angry former employees, social and political activists, vandals, saboteurs, thieves and spies, and domestic and international terrorists are examined. The importance of protecting equipment from potential natural disasters and damaging random events is also covered.

The recommended practices are cumulative and interrelated, which means that the more comprehensive the physical protection program the greater the possibility of reducing damage from a wide array of attacks and events. The practices are listed under threat areas because they are tied to preventing harm caused by the behaviors most characteristic of a specific type of attacker. This is not a perfect categorization but is done to address common behaviors, motivations, and skill sets of the various types of attackers. Please do not ignore the practices because you think there are not threats from specific types of attackers. It is better to take a holistic look at physical security and eliminate as much vulnerability as possible.

Action steps to launch a physical security program for IT equipment, network technology, and telecommunications assets are provided at the end of the chapter. These include how to organize a physical security effort and the initial steps to evaluate physical security in a broad sense, including security for buildings where at-risk equipment is located. The practices examined in this chapter can be evaluated for inclusion in an overall physical security plan, which is discussed in later chapters.

1.1   Why Physical Security Is Important

Physical security is important for several reasons, most of which have a basis in economics. First, equipment is expensive to acquire, install, and integrate into the infrastructure of an organization. Second, the operations of an organization are dependent on the technology infrastructure, which means that disruption of operations quickly turns into unnecessary costs and, when applicable, a potential loss of revenue. Third, laws in most computer-dependent nations require the protection of data and proprietary information stored on computer systems so that if this information is compromised there is a potential for fines or civil litigation.

The potential cost of a one-day (8-hour) outage because centralized servers and network or communications equipment is physically damaged to the point that it requires repair or replacement, can be rather easily calculated. Table 1.1 shows an easy-to-apply formula for deriving potential costs for a one-day outage in an organization that has 100 employees who require access to computers and communications equipment to do their work.

Table 1.1   *Cost of a One-Day Outage*

Variable	Description	Quantity
A	Number of employees who do work that requires access to computers & communications equipment	100
B	Average cost of employee hour including salaries, benefits, facilities, and overhead	$50.00
C	Potential lost productivity for one day of system outages (A * B * 8)	$40,000
D	Cost to restore or replace damaged equipment	???
	Total cost of outage	C + D

The example shows an average cost of an employee hour that includes salaries, benefits, facilities, and overhead costs as $50.00 per hour. Lost productivity could reach $40,000, depending on how much of the work each employee does requires access to computers and communications equipment. To derive the total cost of a one-day outage, the amount of lost productivity is added to the cost to restore or replace damaged equipment.

Table 1.2 shows that in an organization with 200 employees who require access to computers and communications equipment to do their work, the potential cost of a three-day (24 working hours) outage can be as high $240,000 plus the cost to restore or replace damaged equipment.

Table 1.2   *Cost of a Three-Day Outage*

Variable	Description	Quantity
A	Number of employees who do work that requires access to computers & communications equipment	200
B	Average cost of employee hour, including salaries benefits, facilities, and overhead	$50.00
C	Potential lost productivity for one day of system outages (A * B * 24)	$240,000
D	Cost to restore or replace damaged equipment	???
	Total cost of outage	C + D

The potential costs of downtime because of the physical damage to centralized computer and communications equipment will of course be different for every organization. The examples shown in Tables 1.1 and 1.2 can be used to help develop a cost-of-downtime model for your organization. By developing an organization-specific model, physical security planners and managers can help to determine how much could be reasonably spent to better secure computer and communications equipment to avoid outages.

In most cases the cost of downtime will outweigh the cost of improving physical security. However, a return on investment (ROI) analysis is helpful when the cost of improving physical security needs to be justified to decision makers.

1.2   The Relationship Between Physical and Cyber Security

During the last decade there was considerable emphasis placed on improving cyber security. Given the growing threat of malicious code attacks and hacking incidents, improving cyber security generally results in a positive ROI.

It is important to bear in mind that there is a definite relationship between cyber security and physical security of computer and communications equipment, the most obvious being that if an unauthorized individual gains access to an office space with a computer that is logged onto a network, that individual will have equal or greater access to systems than many hackers can achieve. Such access allows individuals to potentially establish unauthorized user accounts, place Trojans or spyware on systems, access protected data, or steal proprietary data. The bottom line here is that no matter how good cyber security is, if an individual can walk into a facility and gain access to systems, that individual has in effect circumvented cyber security defenses.

In addition, laptops that are lost or stolen are all too often equipped with software that is configured for access to host systems. Thus the physical security of mobile computing devices is a weakness that needs to be addressed. Physical security for mobile and remote computing is discussed in later chapters of this book.

Another relationship between physical and cyber security exists when customers, suppliers, or services providers have remote access to a related organization's computer systems. If physical security at the facilities where such computers are located is not adequate, the cyber security of the host computers can be compromised in a manner similar to that described when a trespasser walks into an office and accesses a computer system. Thus it is advisable to design cyber security mechanisms that do not assume that the remote computer has been physically secured.

1.3   Guard Against Disgruntled Employees and Angry Former Employees

Many organizations have suffered damage by disgruntled employees or angry former employees. This is often referred to as the *insider threat*, or *former insider threat*. In situations where employees plan to do damage to the facilities or equipment of an organization, they have several advantages compared to outsiders who want to inflict physical damage, including:

- Knowledge of facility layout and design

- Familiarity with the location of sensitive or expensive equipment

- Duplicate keys that allow them easy access to buildings

- Knowledge of access codes for alarm systems

- The ability to gain access to buildings with the aid of a friend or relative who is still employed by an organization

- Knowledge of organization habits such as shift changes or which doors are not secured during working hours

It may be difficult to neutralize the advantages that disgruntled employees or angry former employees hold if they choose to inflict physical damage. However, Table 1.3 shows some basic steps that can be taken to reduce those advantages.

Table 1.3   *Practices to Reduce Attacks by Employees*

Notify security staff when an employee has been terminated or suspended.
When you do not have a security staff, notify all managers and supervisors when an employee has been terminated or suspended.
Maintain strict policies on access to facilities by nonemployees, and train all employees on those policies.
If terminated or suspended employees had been issued keys, assure that keys are returned.
Change the locks for which any angry former employee had keys.
Change key codes to electronic doors immediately after an employee has been terminated or suspended.
Disable user rights for computers or communications systems held by the former or suspended employee.

1.4   How Activists and Corporate Foes Can Hurt You

Many organizations have also suffered damage by political or social activists. This is often referred to as the *outsider threat*. When activists plan to do damage to the facilities or equipment of an organization they can leverage several advantages, including:

■ They are often highly motivated and intelligent people who plan and organize their attacks well.

■ National or international movements can import people who are experienced at doing damage in support of local groups.

■ The activists who do damage have developed their skills of breaking and entering buildings.

■ The national and international movements often collect considerable amounts of data about an organization that can help them identify specific locations to attack.

■ The experienced activists' attackers are not very concerned about being arrested or prosecuted, which makes laws ineffective as a deterrent.

■ The experienced activists' attackers often take advantage of holidays to launch an attack.

It can be very difficult to neutralize the advantages that experienced and organized social and political activists have if they choose to inflict physical damage. However, Table 1.4 shows some basic steps that can be taken to reduce those advantages.

Table 1.4   *Practices to Reduce Attacks by Activists*

Notify security staff of the activist groups that may have targeted your organization or similar organizations.
When you do not have a security staff, notify all managers and supervisors of the activist groups that may have targeted your organization or similar organizations.
Ensure that the primary services for the building are secured, including electricity, telecommunications, gas, water, and sewer, in a way that makes it difficult to access and harm control systems and connections.
Develop contingency plans for disruptions in primary services.
Determine if critical or sensitive information is stored or handled at the building, and develop contingency plans and recovery plans for operations.
Identify and secure locations of important and expensive equipment.
Minimize the circulation of information to the general public about what activities take place in a facility.
Minimize the profile of activities that take place in a facility by limiting the identification of the facility in scientific papers, press releases, or public mention by researchers or executives about the facility.
If possible, draw attention to other facilities owned by the organization and use those facilities as decoys for activist actions.

1.5   Vandals Who Damage for Fun

Many organizations have also suffered damage by random vandals who do not hold any specific animosities toward an organization. This is often referred to as *random threat*. Situations in which vandals plan to do damage to the facilities or equipment of an organization have several common behaviors, including:

- Vandals are often not deterred by laws against physical destruction or vandalism.

- The activities of vandals are often driven by peer pressure to perform antisocial actions.

- Vandals have little consideration for the effects of their actions.

- Vandals often attack in small groups, using one or more members as scouts to test security.

- Vandals also use one or more members of their groups to perform lookout duties and alert the group of security force or police force arrival and reactions.

- Vandals usually perform random acts of destruction and damage those things that are the easiest targets.

It can be very difficult to stop the behaviors of random vandals if they choose to inflict physical damage. However, Table 1.5 shows some basic steps that can be taken to reduce damages.

Table 1.5   *Practices to Reduce Attacks by Vandals*

Notify security staff of recent or ongoing vandal activity in areas around a facility.
When you do not have a security staff, notify all managers and supervisors of recent or ongoing vandal activity in areas around a facility.
Maintain basic building security functions such as night lighting, closed circuit cameras to monitor activities, and intrusion detection systems that activate alarms to initiate response by private security forces or local police.
Post signs warning of no trespassing and awards for information leading to the arrest of individuals who damage property.
Work with local law enforcement agencies to support community watch programs and other crime reduction efforts.

1.6   Saboteurs Who Work for Profit

Many organizations have suffered damage from professional saboteurs. Unlike random vandals, saboteurs usually hold specific animosities toward an organization or an organization that has facilities adjacent to or near your facilities. Many saboteurs work for financial gain, or in times of war work for a combination of financial gain and political allegiance. Other saboteurs may be part of a larger extortion scheme. When saboteurs plan to do damage to the facilities or equipment of an organization they have several advantages, including:

- Saboteurs for hire are often well-trained individuals who are willing to employ arson or explosive techniques to cause damage.

- Saboteurs often conduct extensive research about organizations and their facilities before they strike.

- Saboteurs are usually skilled at eluding security forces and local law enforcement.

- Saboteurs often strike specific facilities or types of equipment and do so in a manner to cause very targeted and calculated damage.

It can be very difficult to neutralize the advantages of saboteurs who have targeted an organization if they choose to inflict physical damage. However, Table 1.6 shows some basic steps that can be taken to reduce damages.

Table 1.6 *Practices to Reduce Attacks by Saboteurs*

Notify security staff of any known saboteurs who may be targeting your organization.
When you do not have a security staff, notify all managers and supervisors of any known saboteurs who may be targeting your organization.
If a threat of sabotage is detected, hire private investigators to help determine who may be supporting such efforts.
If specific intelligence is gathered about supporting organizations or specific individuals, consider notifying the FBI or other appropriate law enforcement agency.
If specific threats or extortion schemes are detected, consider notifying the FBI or other appropriate law enforcement agency.
As is helpful with dealing with other possible intruders or attackers, the internal layout of a building or facility should not be clearly labeled. (For example, do not post signs on doors to identify things such as telecommunications closets, server rooms, or data processing centers.)
Use key code or other locks to secure areas such as server rooms, telecommunications closets, or data processing centers.
Use surveillance cameras in areas such as server rooms, telecommunications closets, or data processing centers that can record and store images of activities in those areas.

1.7 Thieves and Spies Are Everywhere

Many organizations have suffered damage or theft of intellectual property by thieves and industrial spies. These types of attackers usually do not want to cause damage but prefer to gain access to systems to retrieve and steal data and information. Most such spies work for financial gain and may target a specific organization or organizations that are active in an industry sector in which the thief or spy specializes. Some thieves or spies may also be part of a larger extortion scheme. Thieves or spies planning to steal data or information from an organization have several advantages, including:

- Thieves or spies, like saboteurs, often work for hire and are well-trained individuals who are willing to go to great lengths to obtain the data or information they are seeking.

- Thieves or spies often conduct extensive research about organizations and their facilities before they attempt to steal data or information.

- Thieves or spies are usually skilled at eluding security forces and local law enforcement.

- Thieves or spies often have supporters who pay them well for data and information, which in turn provides them with financial resources to enable long-term operations.

It can be very difficult to neutralize the advantages of thieves or spies who have targeted an organization if they choose to steal data or information. However, Table 1.7 shows some basic steps that can be taken to reduce losses.

Table 1.7 *Practices to Reduce Attacks by Thieves and Spies*

Notify security staff of known thieves or spies who may have targeted your organization.
When you do not have a security staff, notify all managers and supervisors known thieves or spies who may have targeted your organization.
Discuss specific knowledge about known thieves or spies who may have targeted your organization with the FBI or other appropriate law enforcement organization.
Thieves or spies often use social engineering methods to infiltrate or obtain information about an organization, so employees should be trained to not provide information to outsiders.

Table 1.7 *Practices to Reduce Attacks by Thieves and Spies (continued)*

Thieves or spies often use dumpster diving to obtain scraps of information about an organization that can be used in social engineering efforts to obtain further information. This means that you need to be very careful about what you throw in your trash cans and should shred any paper that has any information on it about the organization. Electronic media also should be thoroughly destroyed before disposal.
If computers are left on overnight, users should log off of their systems to reduce ease of access.
Password discipline should also be maintained, and passwords should be complex and changed frequently.

1.8   Domestic Terrorists Are Still a Threat

Defining terrorism is not as easy it sounds. Several agencies of the United States government work with different although somewhat related definitions of terrorism. For the purpose of this analysis, domestic terrorists are considered to include hate groups, extreme militants, or groups opposed to the existence of the nation or society as it is currently organized and structured.

Relatively few organizations have suffered direct damage from the actions of domestic terrorists. However, when damage has occurred it has often been extreme, with the most severe example being the bombing of the United States federal office building in Oklahoma City. In addition to destroying the federal office building, the bombing literally wiped out dozens of surrounding buildings and businesses.

Domestic terrorists are a considerably different type of threat from the other types of attackers mentioned in this chapter. When domestic terrorists plan to do damage to the facilities or equipment of an organization or the facilities of an organization located in a nearby facility, they have several advantages, including:

- Domestic terrorists tend to study vulnerabilities that they can exploit when they plan an attack.

- Domestic terrorists often use extreme measures and have little regard for human life during their attacks.

- Domestic terrorists are not deterred by laws, nor are they compliant with the social norms of the society against which they wish to retaliate.

- Domestic terrorists tend to develop sufficient skills to launch a planned attack.

It can be very difficult to neutralize the advantages of domestic terrorists who have targeted an organization if they choose to inflict harm. However, Table 1.8 shows some basic steps that can be taken to reduce damages.

Table 1.8   *Practices to Reduce Attacks by Domestic Terrorists*

Notify security staff of any specific knowledge about potential domestic terrorist attacks.
When you do not have a security staff, notify all managers and supervisors of any specific knowledge about potential domestic terrorist attacks.
Work with local law enforcement agencies to determine if domestic terrorists are a threat to your organization or organizations with nearby facilities.
If your technology is located in a building with other occupants, conduct your own assessment of the attractiveness of those organizations as targets for domestic terrorists. If you conclude that your technology is located in a building occupied by attractive targets, consider moving it to another location.
Conduct your own assessment of the location of your facility relative to the location of attractive targets such as government buildings, iconic properties, major commercial centers, or major transportation centers. If you conclude that your technology is located close to such targets, consider moving it to another location.
Conduct a vulnerability assessment of your building to terrorist attacks, including how well the building can be secured; structural systems; building envelope; mechanical systems; heating, ventilation, and air conditioning (HVAC); plumbing, gas, and electrical systems; and fire alarm and other security systems. The key question to ask is how accessible are these systems to individuals who would like to do damage? If these systems are too open or cannot be secured, consider hiring an architect for redesign or moving your technology to another location.
Conduct an assessment of the proximity of your facilities to locations that host events, attractions, festivals, celebrations, open-air markets, parades, rallies, demonstrations, marches, or religious services that could be targets of domestic terrorists. If your technology is in a facility that is close to such locations used by groups that have been targeted by domestic terrorists in the past, you should bolster security or consider moving the technology.

Table 1.8   *Practices to Reduce Attacks by Domestic Terrorists (continued)*

Eliminate potential building access through utility tunnels, corridors, manholes, and storm water runoff culverts.
Evaluate the need for barriers to keep out attackers, including passive barriers such as bollards, walls, hardened fences (steel cable interlaced), trenches, ponds/basins, concrete planters, street furniture, plantings, trees, sculptures, and fountains. Also consider active barriers such as pop-up bollards, swing arm gates, and rotating plates and drums.
Evaluate parking and vehicle access systems to determine how close to your building attackers can move a vehicle under normal operating conditions. If vehicles cannot be kept at a reasonable distance, consider redesigning roads and parking lots to keep unauthorized vehicles at least 100 feet away from the building.
Develop and enforce procedures to control internal building parking, underground parking garages, and access to service areas and loading docks.
Minimize opportunities for attackers to conceal packages by keeping hedges, shrubbery, large plants, outdoor furniture, trash receptacles, mailboxes, and newspaper vending machines away from your building.
Ensure that emergency vehicles have access to the building and that fire hydrants are readily accessible if they are needed.
Ensure that critical assets are not near an entrance to the building, including telecommunications equipment, utility closets, and building control systems.
Evaluate the planning and zoning efforts related to future structures that are to be erected near your building. If these efforts will result in increasing the vulnerability of your facility, consider lobbying against the efforts through local political systems.
Develop a suspicious package screening program for deliveries arriving at your facility.
Develop procedures to deal with emergency evacuation and lockdown of equipment in the event of a bomb, chemical, or biological threat.

1.9   International Terrorist Are a Growing Threat

Although attacks by international terrorists against nonmilitary or non-government organizations are not frequent, they can be extremely severe. International terrorists are a considerably different type of threat from domestic terrorists because of their willingness to die during an attack. When international terrorists plan to do damage to the facilities or equipment of an organization, or the facilities of an organization located in a nearby facility, they have several advantages, including:

- Like domestic terrorists, international terrorists also study vulnerabilities that they can exploit when they plan an attack.

- International terrorists mostly rely on extreme measures and have little regard for human life during their attacks.

- International terrorists tend to be driven by hatred for those they are attacking. This is most often rooted in religious or political beliefs, which in turn provide their greatest motivations for attacking.

- In the case of international terrorists supported by religious extremists, those individuals willing to die during an attack are often promised some sort of martyrdom, which helps motivate them to perform an attack.

- Many international terrorists are also rewarded indirectly when their families receive cash or privilege in their communities, which can become another strong motivator for the attacker.

It can be very difficult to neutralize the advantages international terrorists have if they have targeted an organization. However, Table 1.9 shows some basic steps that can be taken to reduce damages.

Table 1.9 *Practices to Reduce Attacks by International Terrorists*

Notify security staff of known threats from international terrorists.
When you do not have a security staff, notify all managers and supervisors of known threats from international terrorists.
Work with local law enforcement agencies to determine if international terrorists are a threat to your organization or organizations with nearby facilities.
Conduct your own assessment of your organization profile and how or why you may become a target of international terrorists.
If your technology is located in a building with other occupants, conduct your own assessment of the attractiveness of those organizations as targets for international terrorists. If you conclude that your technology is located in a building occupied by attractive targets, consider moving it to another location.

Table 1.9   *Practices to Reduce Attacks by International Terrorists (continued)*

Conduct your own assessment of the location of your facility in relationship to government buildings, iconic properties, major commercial centers, or major transportation centers that may be attractive targets for international terrorists. If you conclude that your technology is located close to such targets, consider moving it to another location.
If you receive packages or mail from other countries you need to develop a suspicious package screening program for deliveries arriving at your facility from.
If you receive shipments of goods or raw materials from other countries you need to develop a screening program for containers, boxes, or crates arriving at your facility.
Conduct background checks of your foreign suppliers to determine if they have relationships with known terrorist organizations.
Restrict the information about your organization that you provide to foreign suppliers or customers.
Conduct background checks of visitors from foreign suppliers or customers to determine if they have relationships with known terrorist organizations before the individuals are allowed into your facilities.
Establish a monitoring system to determine if your organization is mentioned on the websites or in the communications of terrorist groups or terrorist sympathizers and supporters.

1.10 Physical Security for Natural Disasters

Physical security for IT assets during natural disasters is especially important in areas where such events are frequent. This includes geographic locations that experience frequent severe weather, tornadoes, hurricanes, earthquakes, fires, snowstorms, or floods.

There are two primary types of protection that must be accomplished in the event of natural disasters. The first is to ensure that the natural disaster in and of itself does not damage IT equipment. The second is to ensure that the equipment is securable if evacuation of a facility or community is required because of the severity of the disaster. The practices shown in Table 1.10 can help reduce the vulnerability of IT assets to natural disasters.

Table 1.10   *Practices to Reduce Damage from Natural Disasters*

Evaluate the physical location of a facility to determine if it is vulnerable to flooding. If the facility is vulnerable, then IT equipment must be located in a place from which it can be removed temporarily or in a place that is the least susceptible to flooding.
Evaluate the physical location of IT assets within a facility to determine if it is vulnerable to leakage in the event of heavy rains or melting snow. If the location is vulnerable, then the facility should be reinforced against leakage or the equipment should be moved to another location within the facility or to another facility.
Develop a removal plan for IT assets in the event that a building is damaged to the point at which it cannot be utilized. This includes disconnecting and packing the equipment, transporting the equipment, and storing or reinstalling the equipment at an alternative location.
Develop procedures to shut down equipment and secure facilities in the event that personnel must be evacuated from a facility for an extended period of time. This should at minimum include disconnecting power and installing protective covering for the equipment.
Establish an offsite backup location to physical protect duplicate media, documentation, and data in the event that the primary location becomes inaccessible or is destroyed.
Integrate these procedures into the emergency response, disaster recovery, and business continuity plans of your organization.

1.11 Physical Security for Random Incidents

Random incidents can include a variety of disruptions, ranging from riots as a result of civil unrest, power blackouts like the one that occurred in August of 2003 in the Northeastern United States and Canada, or unruly celebrations after sporting events. The key thing to keep in mind about being prepared for a random event is that basic procedures need to be developed that will quickly maximize physical security.

The practices shown in Table 1.11 can help reduce the vulnerability of IT assets when a random event creates a threat to IT assets.

Table 1.11 *Practices to Reduce Damage from Random Incidents*

Establish a response plan for your building and IT asset security that can be executed quickly in case of a random incident that threatens a facility or the personnel in that facility.
Establish a notification procedure to inform management that a random incident has disrupted or may disrupt operations.
Establish a notification procedure to inform employees that a random incident has disrupted or may disrupt operations, and instruct them as to what actions they should take.
Rehearse all of the random incident procedures and modify procedures if necessary.
Integrate these procedures into the emergency response, disaster recovery, and business continuity plans of your organization.

1.12   Action Steps to Improve Physical IT Security

The material in this chapter shows basic procedures to reduce the possibility that various types of attackers can succeed in doing physical damage to IT assets. As steps are taken to improve physical security of IT assets, managers, planners, and technical staff should understand the following rudiments:

- There are many types of people who could possibly damage IT assets, all with unique motivations, skill levels, and behaviors that influence how they might attack and the extent of damage they may inflict.

- There is not a single solution to protecting IT assets because it takes several small but related steps to reduce vulnerabilities and decrease the opportunities attackers have to do damage.

- Protecting IT assets requires identifying vulnerabilities within and threats to a facility, the areas around a facility, and in the community in which the facility is located, and then taking steps to reduce those vulnerabilities or eliminate threats.

- Improving the physical security of IT assets is a time-consuming process that will probably take several weeks or even months to accomplish.

There are several steps that organizations can take to help improve the physical security of IT assets. Recommended steps are included at the end of each chapter. The action steps listed in Table 1.12 are designed to help an organization improve physical security of IT assets.

Table 1.12 *Action Steps to Improve Physical IT Security*

Step Number	Action Step
1.01	Establish a working group to evaluate how the organization is addressing the physical security of IT assets.
1.02	Select members of the working group from IT, human resources, legal, and other departments.
1.03	Designate two co-chairs for the working group.
1.04	Convene the working group to discuss how they can best organize themselves to address physical security of IT assets.
1.05	The working group should set a timeline for activities based on the action steps contained in subsequent chapters of this book.
1.06	The working group should create subgroups to examine the practices included in this chapter to determine their applicability to your organization.
1.07	Once the subgroups have determined applicability of practices in this chapter, plans should be formulated for implementation or further study should be conducted when necessary, as stated in the practices.
1.08	Timelines should be established for the studies and adequate time should be allowed for the studies to be conducted. Upon completion, the study groups should report back to the main working group.
1.09	The working group should evaluate the results of any studies conducted and formulate recommendations to management for appropriate changes to existing procedures or the implementation of new procedures.
1.10	When appropriate, the working group should formulate or at least comment on the budgets for building renovations that can help to improve physical security.
1.11	Preserve the research and evaluations done at this phase for use when developing a comprehensive physical IT security plan, as discussed in later chapters.

2

Establishing a Physical IT Security Function

To have effective physical security for IT equipment, network technology, and telecommunications assets, it is important that responsibilities be assigned to staff who are appropriately placed in an organization. An individual in a management position must be responsible for overseeing planning, implementation, and maintenance of plans and procedures. Staff responsible for physical security need to be trained and have their performance evaluated. To simplify establishing a physical IT security function, the following conditions should be considered:

- How existing physical security efforts are managed and staffed
- The financial resources available for new security efforts
- The human resources that are in place for physical security

Action step 1.01 in Chapter 1 called for establishing a working group to evaluate how your organization is addressing the physical security of IT assets and to evaluate and plan alternatives or improvements. The work of the physical security working group can help establish a security function including:

- The organizational placement of the physical IT security function
- Establishing interdepartmental relationships for physical security
- Evaluating financial resources
- Determining the role of corporate security in physical IT security
- Determining the role of cyber security in physical IT security
- Determining the role of network security in physical IT security

- Developing relationships with law enforcement agencies
- Developing relationships with private security providers
- Establishing and utilizing an alert system for incidents

This chapter discusses these aspects of physical IT security and provides action items to enable organizations to move ahead in establishing a function to address physical security needs.

2.1   Organizational Placement of the IT Physical Security Function

There is not a single best solution for establishing a physical IT security function within an organization. There are, however, several factors that influence how this could be accomplished. These include the size of an organization, the existing structure of an organization, and the geographical disbursement of facilities and personnel.

If there is an existing physical security function already established in an organization, then that security function should be evaluated to determine if it is capable of contributing to the development and implementation of physical IT security policies, plans, and procedures. This should not be too difficult to determine if a realistic assessment of existing capabilities can be accomplished. Large organizations often have a division-level manager of security that is responsible for security of facilities, assets, personnel, and intellectual property. Figure 2.1 shows a sample organization chart in which physical IT security responsibilities are performed by a building security manager and an asset security manager. In this case physical IT security needs that are part of building infrastructure or building systems such as locks, alarms, access management, and security cameras can be addressed by the building security manager.

The asset security manager can work to address security needs of specific types of equipment, including asset identification and management or lock-down devices. The dotted line between the IT security function and the building and asset security functions shows that the IT security function provides input on physical security needs.

In smaller organizations the physical security function often is not managed at the division level but is placed under a director of operations and is staffed by a middle manager or supervisory-level employee. Figure 2.2 shows an organization in which physical security responsibilities are managed under business operations.

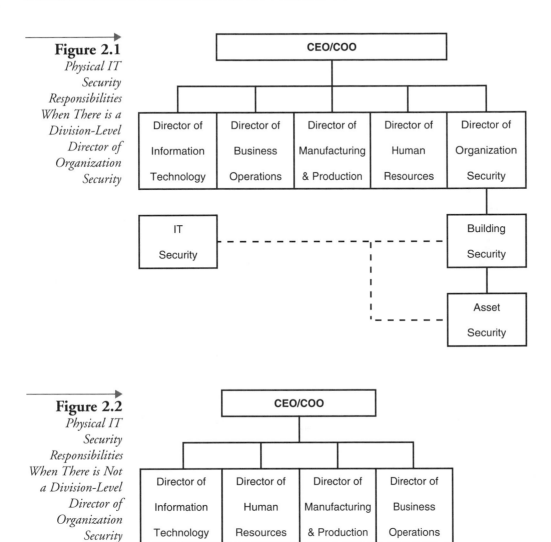

Figure 2.1
Physical IT Security Responsibilities When There is a Division-Level Director of Organization Security

Figure 2.2
Physical IT Security Responsibilities When There is Not a Division-Level Director of Organization Security

In this case the functions that were divided between a building security manager and an asset security manager can most likely be performed by the same person. The dotted line between the IT security function and organization security function indicates that the IT security function provides input on physical security needs.

There are some organizations that do not have a security function at all but still need to have physical IT security procedures. There are as many alternatives as there are organization structures to meet physical IT security needs. In very small organizations, for example, the combined efforts of the IT staff and the office manager can be leveraged to implement physical IT security measures. The key thing to remember is that the goal is to improve physical IT security and not to build a new security department.

2.2   Interdepartmental Relationships for Physical Security

Regardless of where primary responsibility for physical IT security is placed within an organization, many departments need to share responsibilities. In most cases, once plans and procedures have been developed there will not be a need for a dedicated staff person to work full time on physical IT security efforts. Responsibilities can be assigned to existing security staff responsible for building security, asset security, or IT security. One of the major goals of creating the physical IT security working group is to determine how to best distribute responsibilities.

Table 2.1 provides a sample distribution of departmental responsibilities for physical IT security. The roles of corporate security, IT security, and network security are discussed in detail in later sections of this chapter.

Table 2.1   *Departmental Responsibilities for Physical IT Security*

Department	Physical Security Responsibility
Central IT	Advise on procedures that affect data centers and distributed computing and on security technology
Data Network Management	Advise on procedures that affect networking equipment, cabling, WAN connections, and remote computing
Telecommunications	Advise on procedures that affect telecom equipment, voice terminals, and carrier connections
Organization Security	Implement access control procedures, advise on physical security for equipment and facilities
Buildings and Grounds	Install locks, security devices, and access control systems, and maintain security systems
Purchasing	Acquire needed equipment and security systems

Table 2.1 *Departmental Responsibilities for Physical IT Security (continued)*

Legal	Advise on policies and forms that employees sign regarding adherence to policies
Human Resources	Manage training programs, retain signed policy statements of employees
PR and Internal Communications	Promote physical IT security awareness
Manufacturing, Business Operations, and Other Functional or Product-Focused Departments	Assist in implementing physical IT security plans and procedures

2.3   Evaluating Financial Resources

The financial resources to improve physical IT security can come from a variety of sources or departmental budgets. If an organization has a charge-back system for IT services, department-specific physical IT security efforts can be charged directly to departments. These expenses also can be distributed among all departments by including them in overhead charges. Expenses also can be carried by the various departments that have responsibilities for physical IT security, as shown in Table 2.1.

The types of expenses that each department can absorb for initial or ongoing physical IT security efforts are shown in Table 2.2.

Table 2.2 *Financial Responsibilities for Physical IT Security*

Department	**Financial Responsibility**
Central IT	Cost of securing data centers, centralized servers, and staff time for advising other departments on security procedures
Data Network Management	Costs of securing networking equipment, cabling, and WAN connections
Telecommunications	Costs of securing centralized telecom equipment and carrier connections

Table 2.2   *Financial Responsibilities for Physical IT Security (continued)*

Organization Security	Staff time to implement access control procedures and advise on physical security for equipment and facilities
Buildings and Grounds	Costs of locks, security devices, and access control systems, and the costs to install and maintain security systems
Purchasing	Staff time required to acquire needed equipment and security systems
Legal	Staff time to advise on policies and forms that employees sign regarding adherence to policies
Human Resources	Staff time to manage training programs and retain signed policy statements of employees
PR and Internal Communications, Manufacturing, Business Operations, and Other Functional or Product Focused Departments	Staff time and costs of materials to promote physical IT security awareness
	Costs of equipment to secure user terminals, desktop computers, peripherals and voice equipment used in the department as well as remote computing devices used by employees

2.4   The Role of Corporate Security

The role of corporate security in implementing a physical IT security program will vary, depending on the structure of the security department and its ongoing responsibilities. At minimum, corporate security should provide staff time to implement access control procedures and advise on physical security for equipment and facilities. There are several other responsibilities that corporate security could provide, including:

- Conduct ongoing surveillance of facilities and equipment.
- Investigate security incidents such as the theft of equipment or data.
- Conduct or participate in security training.
- Work with central IT department in developing security policies and procedures.
- Provide security for equipment removal during natural disasters.

- Provide mailroom security and package screening.

- Provide loading dock security and vehicle screening.

- Operate central command centers for security or disaster response.

- Manage safe rooms and secure areas for sensitive materials and equipment.

- Manage security and background checks for personnel in sensitive positions.

- Maintain and operate facility or data center access control systems.

- Conduct monthly sweeps for bugs, phone taps, or unauthorized surveillance cameras.

- Enforce no-photo rules and restrictions on cell phones with cameras.

- Prevent employee pilferage.

As the role of corporate security expands, so does the requirement for training security personnel on policies and procedures. You should expect that this training is necessary to improve the effectiveness of security. But regardless of who performs the tasks and functions in the preceding list, it is important to recognize that you must hire appropriately skilled staff and conduct proper training.

2.5   The Role of IT Security

The role of IT security in implementing a physical IT security program will vary, depending on how the capabilities of the corporate security department and the IT security unit complement each other and can be blended into an effective program. At minimum, the IT security staff should advise departments on physical security procedures and help to set requirements for the physical security of data centers, centralized servers, departmental computing resources, desktop systems, and remote and mobile computing devices. Additional work can include:

- Determining levels of security for equipment areas

- Evaluating and selecting products for securing departmental computing resources, desktop systems, and remote and mobile computing devices

- Integrating cyber security efforts with physical security efforts for departmental computing resources, desktop systems, and remote and mobile computing devices

- Installing, maintaining, and operating LAN-based surveillance technology
- Automating access control systems
- Automating equipment inventory systems
- Developing training programs for physical IT security
- Creating computer-based training programs for physical IT security policies and procedures
- Developing plans and procedures for emergency removal of IT equipment
- Installing and maintaining equipment for central control and disaster response centers
- Ensuring that computer-based information relating to security is protected and that access to that information is limited to those employees with a need to know

2.6   The Role of Network Security

The role of network security in implementing a physical IT security program will also vary, depending on the capabilities of the corporate security department and the network security unit. As with the IT security unit, the efforts of the network security unit and the organization security unit should be blended into an effective program.

At minimum, the network security staff should advise departments on physical security procedures and help to set requirements for the physical security of networking equipment, cabling systems, and WAN gateway devices. The network security staff may also be capable of providing assistance for developing security procedures for remote and mobile computing devices. Additional work can include:

- Determining levels of security for network equipment areas
- Evaluating and selecting products for securing networking equipment, cabling systems, and WAN gateway devices
- Integrating cyber security efforts with physical security efforts for networking equipment, cabling systems, and WAN gateway devices
- Installing, maintaining, and operating LAN-based surveillance technology
- Providing network support for the automation of access control systems

- Development of plans and procedures for emergency removal of network equipment

- Installing and maintaining networks for central control and disaster response centers

- Developing training programs for physical IT security

2.7   **Relationships with Law Enforcement**

As was discussed in Chapter 1, physical damage to IT equipment, network technology, and telecommunications assets can be similar to malicious code and hacking attacks in that it can disrupt business operations and severely affect productivity. It can also result in the loss of revenue. In the event that you experience a physical crime against your IT or communications systems, law enforcement agencies recommend that you:

- Follow organizational policies and procedures. (Your organization should have an incident response capability and plan in place.)

- Contact the incident response team for your organization.

- Respond quickly and contact law enforcement.

- Do not disturb the crime scene.

- Establish points of contact with general counsel, emergency response staff, and law enforcement. (Pre-established contacts will help in a quick response effort.)

- Identify a primary point of contact to handle potential evidence. Establish a chain of custody for evidence. (Potential hardware and software evidence that is not properly controlled may lose its value.)

- DO NOT contact the suspected perpetrator.

Compile as much information as possible about the incident. Information that law enforcement investigators will find helpful includes:

- Date, time, and duration of incident

- The name, title, telephone number, fax number, and e-mail address of the point of contact for law enforcement, and the name of your organization, address, city, state, zip code, and country

- The physical locations of computer systems and or networks that have been damaged

- Whether the systems are managed in-house or by a contractor

- Whether the affected systems or networks are critical to the organization's mission

- The nature of the problem, which could include intrusion, system impairment, unauthorized access, compromise of system integrity, theft, or damage

- If the problem has been experienced before

- Suspected method of entry through which the attacker gained access

- The suspected perpetrators and the possible motivations of the attack, which could include an insider or disgruntled employee, former employee, or competitor

- If the suspect is an employee or former employee, you should determine and report the type of facility and computer system access the employee has or had

- What security infrastructure was in place, which could include locks, surveillance cameras, security guards, etc.

- Whether the intrusion or attack resulted in a loss or compromise of sensitive, classified, or proprietary information

- Whether the intrusion or attack resulted in damage to systems or data

It also may be necessary to determine a dollar value of damage, business loss, and cost to restore systems to normal operating conditions. The following information is helpful in determining dollar amounts:

- In the event that repairs or recovery were performed by a contractor, you should determine the charges incurred for services.

- If in-house staff were involved in repairing systems or data and restoring systems to normal operating conditions, you should determine the number of hours staff expended to accomplish these tasks and the hourly wages, benefits, and overhead associated with each employee involved in the recovery.

- If business was disrupted in some way, you should determine the number of transactions or sales that were actually disrupted and their dollar value.

- If systems were impaired to the point that actual disrupted transactions or sales cannot be determined, then you should determine the dollar value of transactions or sales that occur on a comparable day for the duration of the system outage.

- If systems are used to produce goods, deliver services, or manage operations, then determine the value of that disruption. (You may have had similar experiences if operations were disrupted because of inclement weather, fires, earthquakes, or other disruptive incidents.)

- If systems were physically damaged, you need to know what you paid to acquire and install the systems.

- If systems were stolen, you need to know what you paid to acquire and install the systems and the cost of actions taken to ensure that information on the stolen systems cannot be used to access systems.

- If intellectual property or trade secrets were stolen, then you need to determine the value of that property.

- If intellectual property or trade secrets were used by a competitor or other party, then you need to determine the impact on your business.

2.8   Relationships with Private Security Providers

If your organization decides to engage a private security consulting, guard, or officer firm, there are several things you should consider. It is important to make sure you know what you need from such a firm and that you negotiate a solid contract to make sure you do in fact get what you are paying for when you hire a private firm. The following practices are common when hiring a private security firm.

- Check the credentials and references of security consultants.
- Check the references and reputations of security guard and security officer services.
- Evaluate the training standards set by security services for their personnel.
- Assure that all security staff assigned to your facilities have met the training requirements.
- If armed security guards are used, be sure to understand the policies that govern their use of weapons.

- Understand the legal limitations and ramifications for using armed security guards in your city, county, and state.

- Evaluate proposed contracts for security guard services to determine if they meet your expectations and needs.

- Compare costs between competing security guard service companies.

- Evaluate proposed contracts for security consulting services to determine if they meet your expectations and needs. Give special attention to confidentiality and nondisclosure clauses.

2.9 Establishing and Utilizing an Alert System

An internal reporting system for physical security incidents allows employees, customers, and associates to report physical damage. Such reporting systems are an excellent way to quickly identify that an incident has occurred. There are several elements to a successful internal reporting system:

- Employee training on how to report that a physical attack has occurred
- A process for which employees send or file reports
- A process for security staff to receive reports and respond

The security department and other divisions need to work together to design, launch, and support an internal reporting system. The system needs to be easy to use, employees need to be informed about the system and trained to use the system, and above all the system must be responsive. If employees do not feel that the security department is responding to reports and taking them seriously, the system will quickly deteriorate and cease to function. One of the easiest ways to support the reporting system is through the security office or IT help desk. The security office or help desk staff needs to be trained to receive the reports and take the necessary steps to initiate a response.

It is advisable to have multiple ways for an employee to file a report. Email or web-based forms are good options, but they will not work if the employee's computer is not functioning. This means that a telephone contact option should also be available. The key to success in all of the contact systems is to make sure that e-mails, web-based reports, and voicemail systems are checked frequently enough to enable a rapid response.

An incident investigation and report should cover many of the points that would be important to report to law enforcement agencies. However, there are several areas that should be covered that may not be of interest to law enforcement agencies, thus it is strongly recommended that two separate reporting approaches be developed. An internal investigation should cover the following areas:

- When the incident began and how long it lasted
- Which systems were affected
- What the effect of the attack was in terms of downtime or disruption
- Whether the same problem had occurred before and if so, when
- How the incident response team became aware of the incident
- How the incident was responded to
- Whether existing procedures were adequate or require modification
- Whether security vulnerabilities were eliminated as a result of the modifications
- How security vulnerabilities were eliminated
- What, if any, lessons were learned from the incident
- What, if any, procedures should be changed as a result of the incident

It is important that organization managers at all levels understand when a physical IT security incident has occurred. Managers can help inform end-users about the attack and ease workflow problems that may result from the attack. Many organizations have a management notification procedure in place. The means of notification needs to be customized for an organization and should take advantage of existing communications mechanisms. Notifications to management should be straightforward and nontechnical. They should also include an estimate of the magnitude of the expected problem as well as an expected duration of any outages that may result from the incident.

It is also important to notify the person in the organization who is responsible for managing insurance claims. If management decides that the incident is of sufficient magnitude, the decision may be made to file a claim with the organization's insurance company. All of the information used for the internal reporting system will likely be of use to the insurance claim coordinator.

It is important that insurance claims be filed in a timely manner. This is especially true if the insurance company wants to send a claims adjuster to evaluate damage prior to the beginning of restoration work.

2.10   Action Steps to Improve Physical IT Security

The material in this chapter examines many of the issues that must be addressed to establish, staff, and fund a physical IT security program. As steps are taken to improve physical security of IT assets, managers, planners, and technical staff should understand the following concepts:

- A physical IT security program requires the cooperative efforts of several departments in an organization.
- Funding for a physical IT security program can be extracted from the budgets of participating departments or charged back in an IT services fee.
- The corporate security, IT security, and network security units of an organization play major roles in a physical IT security program.
- There are several important things to consider when hiring a private security guard, officer, or consultant service.

There are several steps that organizations can take to help improve the physical security of IT assets. Recommended steps are included at the end of each chapter. The action steps listed in Table 2.3 are designed to help an organization determine how best to establish, staff, and fund a physical IT security program.

Table 2.3   *Action Steps to Improve Physical IT Security*

Step Number	Action Step
2.01	Evaluate how responsibilities for physical IT security can be assigned to staff and distributed among various departments.
2.02	Evaluate how economic responsibilities for physical IT security can be distributed among various departments.
2.03	Evaluate the role that corporate security can perform in the development and support of a physical IT security effort.

Table 2.3 *Action Steps to Improve Physical IT Security (continued)*

Step Number	Action Step
2.04	Evaluate the role that IT security can perform in the development and support of a physical IT security effort.
2.05	Evaluate the role that network security can perform in the development and support of a physical IT security effort.
2.06	Evaluate existing procedures for working with law enforcement by comparing those procedures to the practices discussed in this chapter. Prepare recommendations to management on how procedures should be modified or what new procedures should be implemented.
2.07	Evaluate the need for security guards, officers, and consultants. Prepare an analysis for management on how these services may be useful to your organization.
2.08	Evaluate internal reporting and alert systems by comparing procedures to the practices discussed in this chapter. Prepare recommendations to management on how procedures should be modified or what new procedures should be implemented.
2.09	The working group should convene and review the evaluations recommended in the preceding action steps and make recommendations to management for implementation.

3

Developing an IT Physical Security Plan

In January 2000, the Critical Infrastructure Assurance Office of the United States government released a guidebook entitled *Practices for Securing Critical Information Assets*. Physical security involves the protection of building sites and equipment (and information and software contained therein) from theft, vandalism, natural and manmade disasters, and accidental damage.

Managers must be concerned with building construction, room assignments, emergency procedures, regulations governing equipment placement and use, energy and water supplies, product handling, and relationships with employees, outside contractors, and agencies. Some solutions may require the installation of key locks, fire extinguishers, surge protectors, window bars, automatic fire equipment, and alarm systems. This chapter examines the process of developing physical security plans that will encompass all of these requirements.

The types of threats that must be addressed were covered in Chapter 1. Alternative methods on how to organize a physical IT security program were covered in Chapter 2. This chapter examines the basic aspects of the physical IT security planning process including:

- An overview of the planning process
- Developing the IT physical security plan
- Utilizing existing risk exposure analysis
- Integrating physical IT security and cyber security planning
- Integrating physical IT security and disaster recovery planning
- Integrating physical IT security and business continuity planning
- Working with your insurance company
- Establishing an incident response team

Developing a physical IT security plan does not need to be complicated. As was shown in Chapter 2, there are several ways to staff and implement physical IT security needs without establishing a specialized unit or adding several new staff members to existing security efforts. The same approach will be taken in this chapter as the planning process and relationships between existing efforts are examined.

3.1   Overview of the Planning Process

The key to keeping planning expenses down is to leverage existing knowledge and planning efforts in an organization. The action steps included at the end of each chapter are designed to take an organization through the development and implementation process on a step-by-step basis. You should use the action steps that most apply to your organizational structure and culture. The goal is to reduce vulnerabilities as much as possible without spending a great deal of money or consuming excessive staff hours. To help reduce confusion you should follow these simple steps:

1.   Have the physical IT security working group become familiar with the type of threats that need to be addressed (see Chapter 1). Select appropriate action steps from Chapter 1.

2.   Give thought to how you will establish a physical IT security function and take the appropriate action steps in Chapter 2.

3.   Organize your planning process as outlined in this chapter and take the appropriate action steps.

4.   Determine which of the major elements of a plan you need to develop (elements are explained in Chapter 4) and take the appropriate action steps.

5.   Develop and document physical IT security methods and procedures as described in Chapter 5.

6.   Devise an auditing and testing process for procedures as described in Chapter 6.

7.   Tune your incident response process following the guidelines in Chapter 7.

8.   Develop and implement a training program for physical IT security as explained in Chapter 8.

9.   Always keep an eye on the future as your organization changes, expands, adds new facilities, remodels, or closes existing facilities as explained in Chapter 9.

If you followed the action steps in Chapters 1 and 2 you are well on your way to developing your physical IT security plan. First and foremost, you have established a working group before your evaluation activities get underway. The reason that the chapters are in their current order is that the evaluation work and questions addressed in Chapters 1 and 2 help to set the scope of your work from here to the completion of your plan.

Action step 1.06 calls for the working group to create subgroups to examine the practices included in Chapter 1 to determine their applicability to your organization. You should have determined which of those practices are important to your organization and can start focusing efforts on developing procedures. You can, at least until things change, not spend time focusing on areas that are not deemed necessary.

Action step 1.09 calls for the working group to evaluate the results of the studies they conducted and formulate recommendations to management for appropriate changes to existing procedures or the implementation of new procedures. If procedures are already in place and just need to be modified to achieve improvements in security, much of the basic work may be done by now. On the other hand, if there were not procedures in place, then you can start developing those procedures in accordance to the process outlined in the next chapter.

Of course the most expedient situation is one in which an organization has procedures that can be modified to improve security. If that is not the case in your organization, bear in mind that action step 1.11 called for the preservation of the research and evaluations done at that phase for use when developing a comprehensive physical IT security plan as discussed in later chapters. Such preservation will keep you from having to redo the work.

Action step 2.01 called for an evaluation of how responsibilities for physical IT security can be assigned to staff and distributed among various departments. There is not a one-solution-fits-all for making this decision. The tasks and activities outlined in Chapter 2 may be spread across your organization in a very different way than in other organizations.

If you have made the decisions about who will have what responsibilities for physical IT security then you can solidify your planning team. Representatives from the various departments that will be assigned responsibilities for security should participate in the planning process and join your physical IT security working group.

A closely related action step is 2.02, which calls for an evaluation of how economic responsibilities for physical IT security can be distributed among various departments. If you have made these decisions, then much of the funding you need may already be in place. Thus you can start to implement new procedures and purchase new equipment if necessary.

Being realistic about money allows you to realize that not all of the departments will have money in their budgets needed for purchasing equipment or paying for physical changes in facilities to improve security. Do not panic about this. Your plan will not come to fruition overnight and you can add money to budgets for large expenditures in a manner that is consistent with your usual budget cycles. One of the purposes of the various evaluations is to determine what you need. You can always put things into place in an orderly manner as time goes by.

The other action steps in Chapter 2 that call for the evaluations of various security needs and alternatives can be taken as you develop the plan and assess alternatives. Unless there is an immediate threat that must be addressed, it is best to take your time to deal with big and expensive decisions such as hiring outside service firms to help with security.

Another area that does not need to wait until the plan is completed is in action step 2.08 which is an evaluation of internal reporting and alert systems. If you already have such a system in place then your task should be to make sure that the alert and reporting system addresses needs related to physical IT security. If you do not have an alert and reporting system in place you can make immediate recommendations to management about what new procedures should be implemented. However, in the absence of incidents this recommendation also can be integrated in to developing the comprehensive plan for physical IT security.

3.2   Developing the IT Physical Security Plan

The first step is to solidify your decision about the assignment of responsibilities across departments. Once that is done then you should designate the representatives from each of those departments who will work on the development process.

Once the representatives have been designated, convene the newly composed working group along with the results of any evaluations that were done in the action steps in Chapters 1 and 2.

Two co-chairs should be designated at this point. Those co-chairs should have ongoing responsibility for security and IT management. This is recommended because these departments will play a more intensive role in the ongoing management of physical IT security and they probably have the most relevant expertise. Representatives from other departments will certainly play a significant role as time goes by, but for the most part those will be to support the overall process with their specific areas of expertise.

It is important to allocate adequate time for developing the plan and procedures. This includes time to conduct the various evaluations, hold meetings, document procedures, test procedures, and conduct training. The co-chairs should be assigned support staff which can handle arranging meetings and creating documentation. This will likely be a part-time job in most organizations. However, if more staff support is needed bear in mind that the requirement for support will decrease if not end completely once the plan and procedures are developed.

From this point on it is important to maintain momentum. It is easier to keep moving ahead than it is to start and stop the planning and evaluation activities. One word of caution: there are some people in the world who have an irritating tendency to hold excessive meetings in which little if anything is accomplished. Resist this! Do not waste time and do not de-motivate the staff working on the plan by overburdening them with unnecessary meetings.

3.3   Utilizing Existing Risk Exposure Analysis

Many large organizations already have conducted some type of risk exposure analysis. This could have been done for insurance purposes, during the course of disaster recovery or business continuity planning, or for long-term strategic planning purposes. Instead of conducting a new risk exposure analysis, the physical IT security working group should utilize any and all of the existing risk exposure analyses that already have been completed.

By evaluating existing risk exposure analyses security planners will better understand how the organization views risks. The security working group may also be able to identify goals or standards that physical security planning should meet in order to mitigate the risks that an organization faces.

Risk exposure analyses are performed at a variety of levels and should not be confused with detailed vulnerability analyses. Table 3.1 shows various

Table 3.1   *Types of Risk Exposure Analyses*

Type of Analysis	Level of Detail Applicable to Security Planning
Competitive strategy and market position analysis that provides details on the position of an organization relative to existing and future competition	Can include analysis of the impact of business disruption and help illustrate the value and the ROI for mitigation efforts

Table 3.1   *Types of Risk Exposure Analyses (continued)*

Type of Analysis	Level of Detail Applicable to Security Planning
Business continuity plans that provide details on how the organization plans to assure continuance of operations if major events occur or there are drastic economic shifts	Can include analysis of potential geographical shifts in operations or manufacturing and alternatives for managing human resources and intellectual property
Risk management for insurance planning and purchasing that has estimates of how much money policies will pay if various types of losses occur	Can include estimates of value of assets and the impact of business disruption, as well as details on the importance of various facilities
Disaster recovery plans that generally include considerable detail about operations and how business processes will be restored	Can illustrate the relative importance of various assets and show which assets, systems, and operations are critical to business functions
Organization security plans that include threat analysis and details on how security is managed, as well as existing security procedures	Can illustrate types of threats that need to be guarded against and provide details on what types of procedures exist and those that may be lacking
Compliance plans for industries in regulated industries that show the requirements or standards that must be met	Can include details on what security procedures may be required to maintain compliance

types of risk exposure analyses and how they can be used by the physical IT security working group when developing plans and procedures.

Note that the content of the various types of plans and analyses listed below will vary by organization as well as when and how they were performed. The explanation of the level of detail applicable to security planning is provided to illustrate possible contributions to the security planning process rather than an absolute definition of what is included in a specific type of analysis.

3.4   Integrating Physical IT Security and Cyber Security Planning

The conceptual importance of the relationship between cyber security and physical IT security was introduced in Chapter 1. The physical IT security working group should have a representative from the IT security department who has a thorough understanding of the organization's cyber security plan, methods, and procedures.

It is critical that the cyber security plan and the physical IT security plan are synchronized and integrated. This is not a complicated task. A basic rule of thumb can be applied: if a computer or networking application is a priority for cyber protection it should be a priority for physical protection.

The physical IT security work group can save the time and effort required to analyze systems for physical security needs by accepting the analysis that has already been done to determine cyber security priorities.

Figure 3.1 illustrates the process of identifying applications that have high priorities for cyber security, applying high levels of importance for physical security to the equipment that supports the applications, and implementing symmetrical physical security measures.

3.5   Integrating Physical IT Security and Disaster Recovery Planning

The classification of critical applications and systems that is done to set priorities for disaster recovery can provide guidance for setting priorities for physical IT security. This is similar to aligning cyber security and physical security priorities. A basic rule of thumb can be applied: if a computer or

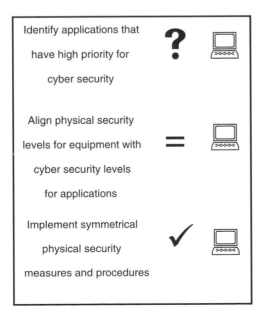

Figure 3.1
*Mapping Cyber
and Physical
Security Priorities*

networking application is critical for disaster recovery, then it should be a priority for physical protection.

The physical IT security work group can save the time and effort required to analyze systems for physical security needs by accepting the analysis that has already been done to determine disaster recovery priorities. It should be noted that most disaster recovery plans are facility specific and the working group may need to review numerous disaster recovery plans in order to align physical IT security with disaster recovery priorities at all of the facilities owned or operated by your organization.

Figure 3.2 illustrates the process of identifying applications and systems that have critical rankings for disaster recovery, applying high levels of physical security to the equipment that supports the applications, and implementing symmetrical physical security measures.

3.6   **Integrating Physical IT Security and Business Continuity Planning**

Relative to disaster recovery planning, few organizations have developed business continuity plans. It is advisable, however, that if your organization does have a business continuity plan the physical IT security working group should review the plan to ensure that necessary physical security is implemented for

Figure 3.2

Mapping Disaster Recovery and Physical Security Priorities

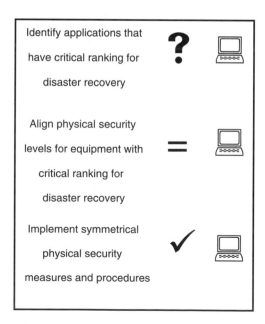

the identified systems. One very practical example is if an organization has designated a facility in another state as the primary fallback site for continuity of operations, then that facility should be equipped to provide appropriate physical IT security for the same type of equipment and systems being protected at the primary facility.

A similar basic rule of thumb can be applied: if a computer or networking application is critical for business operations at one site then it should be a priority for physical protection at fallback sites.

It should be noted that most business continuity plans are enterprisewide, but many are developed for specific lines of business. Thus the working group may need to review numerous business continuity plans to align physical IT security with business continuity strategies.

Figure 3.3 illustrates the process of identifying applications and systems that have been designated as important to business continuity strategies, applying high levels of physical security to the equipment that supports the applications, and implementing symmetrical physical security measures.

3.7   **Working with Your Insurance Company**

Analysis of insurance policies can help establish requirements for physical IT security in two ways. First, insurance policies may set minimum requirements for security before the insured is eligible for coverage. Second, insurance

Figure 3.3
Mapping Continuity and Physical Security Priorities

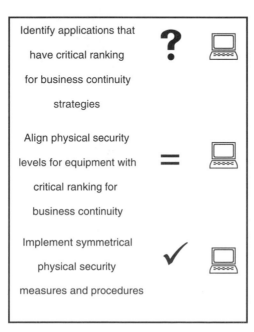

Identify applications that have critical ranking for business continuity strategies

Align physical security levels for equipment with critical ranking for business continuity

Implement symmetrical physical security measures and procedures

companies may offer various discounts on premiums if specific types of security mechanisms are put into place.

With the assistance of the insurance manager, the physical IT security working group should evaluate both of these aspects of your organization's insurance policies. This can yield two possible benefits. First, it will help to ensure that your organization is complying with insurance policy requirements. Second, it may actually help reduce your insurance costs if new opportunities for discounts are identified.

Figure 3.4 illustrates the process of identifying applications or systems that have requirements for protection under insurance policies or where discounts can be obtained by implementing security practices, applying high levels of physical security to the equipment that supports the requirements or advantages, and implementing symmetrical physical security measures.

3.8   Evaluating Regulatory Requirements

There is an ever-growing list of legal and regulatory requirements regarding the security of data and information. Recent laws that affect your organization include the Gramm-Leach-Bliley Act, the Fair Credit Reporting Act, the Health Insurance Portability and Accountability Act, the Children's Online Privacy Protection Act, and the EU Data Protection Directive (as well as EU members' state laws and the Safe Harbor negotiated between the United

Figure 3.4

Mapping Insurance Needs and Physical Security Priorities

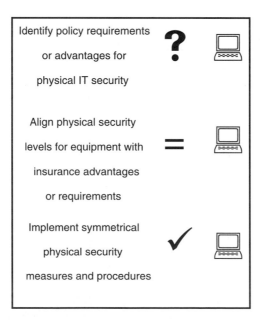

States and the European Union). The best thing you can do to evaluate the actions you need to take to comply with these requirements is to have your legal counsel advise you.

You can also check directly with federal agencies that regulate activities in your business sector. The FTC is one of many federal regulatory agencies that has authority to enforce financial privacy laws. The federal banking agencies, the Securities and Exchange Commission, and the Commodity Futures Trading Commission have jurisdiction over banks, thrifts, credit unions, brokerage firms, and commodity traders. In addition, state insurance authorities also have regulatory authority that may affect your security requirements.

The Gramm-Leach-Bliley Act (GLB Act), which is designed to protect consumer financial privacy, provides a good model for compliance requirements. Its provisions limit when a financial institution may disclose a consumer's nonpublic personal information to nonaffiliated third parties. The law covers a broad range of financial institutions, including many companies not traditionally considered to be financial institutions because they engage in certain financial activities. In addition, any entity that receives consumer financial information from a financial institution may be restricted in its reuse and redisclosure of that information.

Disclosure can be either purposeful or accidental. If your website is hacked and information is compromised, your organization is still responsible for that disclosure. If somebody breaks into your building and steals a computer with this type of data stored on it, you are still responsible for the disclosure.

An overview of the privacy requirements of the GLB Act is available online at the FTC's website, at www.ftc.gov/privacy/glbact/index.html. This guide provides more detailed information than in the overview, to help you comply with the privacy rule's requirements for protecting consumer financial information. It was written for businesses that provide financial products or services to individuals for personal, family, or household use.

The privacy rule protects a consumer's nonpublic personal information (NPI). NPI is any personally identifiable financial information that a financial institution collects about an individual in connection with providing a financial product or service, unless that information is otherwise publicly available. NPI is:

- Any information an individual gives you to get a financial product or service (for example, name, address, income, Social Security number, or other information on an application)

- Any information you get about an individual from a transaction involving your financial product(s) or service(s) (for example, the fact that an individual is your consumer or customer, account numbers, payment history, loan or deposit balances, and credit or debit card purchases)

- Any information you get about an individual in connection with providing a financial product or service (for example, information from court records or from a consumer report)

NPI does not include information that you have a reasonable basis to believe is lawfully made publicly available. In other words, information is not NPI when you have taken steps to determine:

- That the information is generally made lawfully available to the public
- That the individual can direct that it not be made public and has not done so

Publicly available information includes federal, state, or local government records made available to the public, such as the fact that an individual has a mortgage with a particular financial institution. It also includes information that is in widely distributed media such as telephone books, newspapers, and websites that are available to the general public on an unrestricted basis, even if the site requires a password or fee for access.

The GLB Act prohibits financial institutions from sharing account numbers or similar access numbers or codes for marketing purposes. This prohibition applies even when a consumer or customer has not opted out of the disclosure of NPI concerning the account. The prohibition applies to disclosures of account numbers for an individual's credit card account, deposit account, or transaction account to any nonaffiliated third party to use in telemarketing, direct mail marketing, or other marketing through electronic mail to any consumer. A transaction account is any account to which a third party may initiate a charge. This provision does not prohibit the sharing of an encrypted account number if the third party receiving the information has no way to decode it.

The FTC has developed Safeguards Rule for all areas of operation, including three areas that are particularly important to information security: employee management and training, information systems, and managing system failures. The FTC recommends that you store records in a secure area and that you make sure only authorized employees have access to the area. Examples of FTC recommendations include:

- Store paper records in a room, cabinet, or other container that is locked when unattended.

- Ensure that storage areas are protected against destruction or potential damage from physical hazards such as fire or floods.

- Store electronic customer information on a secure server that is accessible only with a password—or has other security protections and keep the server in a physically secure area.

- Do not store sensitive customer data on a machine with an Internet connection.

- Maintain secure backup media and keep archived data secure, for example, by storing offline or in a physically secure area.

- Hire or designate a records retention manager to supervise the disposal of records containing nonpublic personal information.

- Shred or recycle customer information recorded on paper and store it in a secure area until a recycling service picks it up.

- Erase all data when disposing of computers, diskettes, magnetic tapes, hard drives, or any other electronic media that contain customer information and effectively destroy the hardware.

- Have and follow a written contingency plan to address any breaches of your physical, administrative, or technical safeguard.

The FTC also recommends that organizations train employees to take basic steps to maintain physical security of customer information including:

- Locking rooms and file cabinets where paper records are kept
- Using password-activated screensavers
- Using strong passwords (at least eight characters long)
- Changing passwords periodically
- Not posting passwords near employees' computers

Another important legislative action is the Health Insurance Portability and Accountability Act (HIPAA). It requires several types of physical safeguards for information systems. The security standards are focused on preventing unauthorized individuals from gaining access to electronic information. Five areas of physical safeguards include:

- Officially assigned security responsibility for information security

- Media controls including formal procedures for controlling and tracking the handling of hardware and software, and for data backup, storage, and disposal

- Physical access controls including developing a facility security plan, and setting up disaster recovery, emergency modes, and other access and handling controls

- Workstation use policies and procedures to prevent unauthorized access to protected information on workstations and terminals

- Security awareness training for all employees and others with physical access to protected health information

3.9   Action Steps to Improve Physical IT Security

The material in this chapter shows how to move forward in developing physical IT plans and procedures. As steps are taken to improve physical security of IT assets, managers, planners, and technical staff should understand the following rudiments:

- Aligning physical IT security efforts with cyber security plans, disaster recovery plans, and business continuity plans makes sense and can save time during the planning process.

- The physical IT security working group should feel comfortable relying on existing risk exposure analyses to help determine physical IT security priorities.

- Aligning physical IT security practices with minimum requirements set in insurance policies may help ensure that assets are eligible for coverage.

- Aligning physical IT security practices with practices that provide various discounts on premiums may help to reduce insurance costs.

- There are numerous laws and regulations that may require general or specific physical IT security practices with which you may need to comply.

There are several steps that organizations can take to help improve the physical security of IT assets. Recommended steps are included at the end of each chapter. The action steps listed in Table 3.2 are designed to help an organization focus physical IT security planning efforts.

Table 3.2 *Action Steps to Improve Physical IT Security*

Step Number	Action Step
3.01	Finalize the decision about how responsibilities for physical IT security will be distributed across departments.
3.02	Finalize, or at least solidify, the decision about how economic responsibilities for physical IT security will be distributed across departments.
3.03	Assign new members to the physical IT security working group from all of the departments that will have some responsibility for implementing the new physical IT security plan.
3.04	Convene the working group and designate two co-chairs to lead the reconstituted physical IT security working group.
3.05	Evaluate the organization's various risk exposure analyses to determine their usefulness in the planning process as well as any goals or standards that physical security planning should meet to mitigate the risks that an organization faces.
3.06	Evaluate insurance policies to ensure that your physical IT security practices are consistent with minimum requirements set in insurance policies.
3.07	Evaluate insurance policies to determine if there are physical IT security practices that can result in discounts on premiums and may help to reduce insurance costs.
3.08	Evaluate laws and regulations that may require general or specific physical IT security practices with which you may need to comply.
3.09	Assemble all of these evaluations and prepare to move on to the next phase of physical IT security planning and procedure development.

4

Major Elements of a Physical IT Security Plan

At this point you should have selected a solid physical IT security working group and be ready to move ahead in developing and documenting specific procedures for the protection of your IT assets. In addition to the representatives from departments who will have responsibility for various procedures, you should have also designated administrative support staff who will actually create necessary documentation. To start this process you can review the checklist in Table 4.1 to determine the status of the various elements you need to complete the process.

Table 4.1   *Elements Required for Plan Completion*

Element	Status (completed, pending, not applicable)
Departmental responsibilities for plan elements or implementing procedures (Chapter 2)	Enter status for each area in this column.
Reviews of applicable practices included in Chapter 1	
Detailed evaluation of the role that corporate security can perform to support physical IT security efforts (Chapter 2)	
Detailed evaluation of the role that IT security can perform to support of a physical IT security efforts (Chapter 2)	
Detailed evaluation of the role that network security can perform to support physical IT security efforts (Chapter 2)	

Table 4.1 *Elements Required for Plan Completion (continued)*

Element	Status (completed, pending, not applicable)
Detailed evaluation of existing procedures for working with law enforcement (Chapter 2)	
Detailed evaluation of the need for security guards, officers, and consultants (Chapter 2)	
Detailed evaluation of internal reporting and alert systems (Chapter 2)	
Detailed evaluations of various risk exposure analyses including the cyber security plan, disaster recovery plan, and business continuity plan that indicate what must be done to align the physical IT security plan with other risk mitigation efforts (Chapter 3)	
Evaluations of insurance policy requirements and opportunities for discounts in premiums by implementing specific physical IT security practices (Chapter 3)	
Evaluations of laws and regulations that may require general or specific physical IT security practices with which you may need to comply (Chapter 3)	

One of the worst things that can happen to your physical IT security effort is that you work hard to develop a good plan and procedures and create a document that nobody can use or understand. When creating the physical IT security procedures there are a few things that will help make the documentation easier to use and maintain, including:

- Start sections, subsections, and each detailed procedure on a new page so that pages can be updated, printed, and inserted, without reprinting the entire document.

- Maintain a computer-based version of the document that can be accessed with a browser.

- Use straightforward language when writing the document to make it easy to read for a wide variety of people.

- Use at least 12-point fonts so people do not have to strain to read the print.

- Have a person who is not involved with the development of the document read it completely to help make sure that it is understandable by people who are not familiar with the content.

- If procedures are developed to make your organization compliant with legal or regulatory requirements, note which procedure is related to which requirement.

- If procedures are developed to support cyber security, disaster recovery, or business continuity efforts, note which procedure is related to the specific elements of applicable plans.

- In the footer of the documents include the date that each subsection was last updated.

- In each procedure it should be explained in detail which department is responsible for implementing the procedure.

It is also advisable to provide a detailed table of contents for your documentation. This should include a chapter or section title along with a title of each subsection and a list of each procedure that is included in that subsection. When the document is published in an electronic format, it is advisable to hyperlink the table of contents entries to the corresponding section of the document. A sample outline for a physical IT security document is as follows:

1.   Overview and Mission Statement

2.   Organizational Responsibilities

3.   Duty Officers

4.   Contact Lists

5.   Security Procedures for Data Centers

6.   Security Procedures for Wiring and Cabling

7.   Security Procedures for Remote Computers

8.   Security Procedures for Desktops

9.   Security Procedures for Department-Based Servers

10. Security Procedures for Telecom and Datacom Equipment

11. Security Procedures for Manufacturing Control Equipment

12. Security Procedures for Surveillance and Alarm Systems

13. Supporting Documents

Even though there may be some redundance in procedures for the different areas, it is advisable to structure the document in accordance with these sections. The structure is consistent with a typical division of responsibility for the different types of technology. If you separate the procedures in this manner there will be less confusion for the specialized reader. It is easier for people to relate to the types of technology they work with than it is for them to relate to the type of procedure they need to follow.

4.1 Overview and Mission Statement

The mission statement for the physical IT security plan does not need to be lofty or complex. Just get to the point. You should include explanations of other plans or legal and regulatory requirements that the physical IT security plan supports or complements. If procedures are developed to make your organization compliant with legal or regulatory requirements you should indicate with which laws or regulations the plan is designed to comply. If procedures are developed to support cyber security, disaster recovery, or business continuity efforts you should indicate which of those plans the physical IT security plan supports.

It is also advisable to indicate who worked on developing the plan. This will provide future readers with the names of people they can contact to discuss any questions or concerns they may have about the plan.

4.2 Organizational Responsibilities

This section should provide sufficient detail to inform the reader which department performs which tasks and executes which procedures in the plan. Table 4.2 shows a sample chart of responsibilities. The departments listed in the left column are shown only as examples. The short title and applicable procedure number should be listed in the right column. The procedure numbers, if used in your documents, should also be listed in the table of contents.

Table 4.2 *Sample Chart of Responsibilities*

Department	Physical Security Responsibility (each procedure should be listed)
Central IT	
Data Network Management	

Table 4.2 *Sample Chart of Responsibilities (continued)*

Department	Physical Security Responsibility (each procedure should be listed)
Telecommunications	
Organization Security	
Buildings and Grounds	
Purchasing	
Legal	
Human Resources	
PR and Internal Communications	
Manufacturing	
Business Operations	
Other Functional or Product-Focused Departments	

4.3 Duty Officers

Many organizations have adopted the use of duty officers (DOs). The DO has responsibility for making or coordinating management decisions. In general, the business hours DO, or lead manager, is the COO or CEO. In their absence, another manager is assigned the responsibility for acting on behalf of management when operational or emergency decisions must be made. In some cases a DO is also designated at the division level when the highest level division manager is not present. A DO list and assignment system is generally maintained by the central administrative office.

The physical IT security plan, like the cyber security plan, should specify to which manager incidents should be reported. If reporting is to be done through a DO system, then the procedures should specify how the DO should be contacted. There also should be a procedure for reporting to management in the event that the DO becomes unreachable.

The main goal of reporting incidents to management is to facilitate rapid response to the incident and to properly decide if law enforcement agencies should be called in to investigate. The procedures should be well documented so that the IT staff or security staff does not have to improvise in order to notify management.

4.4 Contact Lists

The inclusion of contact lists in a security plan, or in any type of plan for that matter, is both a benefit and a challenge. On the benefit side, the individuals who actually reference the documentation will have a ready list of who is responsible for what along with their contact information. The challenge is not in creating the initial list, but in maintaining the list to make sure it is current both in terms of whom to contact and how to contact them.

Organization security personnel and IT staff have a variety of plans, manuals, procedures, and lists they need to refer to every day. If each of these documents has a list that needs to be updated, the process of managing current information may quickly become impractical for many organizations.

An alternative approach to maintaining individual lists is to have a centralized contact list for a wide range of purposes and incidents. The centralized list could be cross-indexed by contact person and that person's responsibilities. The lists also should indicate the type of incidents or activities for which a contact or notification should be made. The centralized list may be a bit more cumbersome to create the first time around, but once it is established it will likely be easier to maintain in the long run. Such a list should include the following information:

- Type of problem or incident
- Primary contact name, title, and means of contact
- Secondary contact name, title, and means of contact
- Information that should be made available to the contact about the problem or incident

4.5 Security Procedures for Data Centers

Establishing procedures for physical data center security is one of the top priorities when developing a physical IT security plan. The complexity of this section will depend on several different data center characteristics, including whether the data center occupies an entire building or just part of a building. Security procedures that should be addressed for data centers are shown Table 4.3. The table is designed to be used as a checklist to determine if all of the necessary areas have been covered once documentation of procedures has been completed. The checklist can also be used as a guide by the physical IT security working group during their review of the drafted procedures.

Table 4.3 *Checklist for Data Center Security Procedures*

Types of Procedures Needed	Status (completed, pending, not applicable)
If the data center occupies the entire building, then the plan needs to address security for the exterior of the building, lobby areas, utility areas, loading docks, offices, and each subarea of the rooms in which there is IT equipment.	Enter status for each area in this column.
If the data center occupies only part of a building, then the plan needs to address security for IT staff offices and each subarea of the rooms in which there is IT equipment.	
Access control and access management are key elements of a data center security plan and should indicate who has access, how access is granted, how visitors and vendors are managed, and how to deal with breaches of access policies.	
How and when should a lead security officer or manager regularly review access reports?	
What are the procedures for securing selected equipment, cabling systems, encryption equipment, media rooms, and storage cabinets or areas that contain the most sensitive types of information?	
List security methods for utility systems, including air-conditioning, power supplies, network connections, and emergency power systems.	
List security procedures for business-hour operations, after-hour operations, and emergency operations.	
How are up-to-date logs of all equipment managed, which includes serial numbers and configuration information?	
How are up-to-date lists of personnel authorized to access sensitive areas managed?	
How are environmental settings in equipment rooms maintained?	
How are incoming and outgoing equipment, documents, and supplies signed in and out?	
How and where are incoming packages inspected and opened before contents are brought into the data center?	

Table 4.3   *Checklist for Data Center Security Procedures (continued)*

Types of Procedures Needed	Status (completed, pending, not applicable)
How and where are fire suppression systems installed?	
What type of protective containers should be used for sensitive material, including fire-resistant or burglar-resistant standards?	
How are printed materials and used magnetic media disposed of and who is responsible for the disposal?	
If closed-circuit monitors are used, procedures are needed for their use and maintenance.	

4.6   Security Procedures for Wiring and Cabling

Wiring and cabling, especially that which is located outside of the data center, needs to be protected to prevent unauthorized access. This will help prevent wire tapping, intentional damage, and accidental damage during remodeling or building maintenance. Only authorized personnel should have access to the controlled wiring and cabling areas. In addition, wiring and cabling should not be located in areas that serve other functions such as conduits for plumbing or air-conditioning and heating systems.

Standards should be set for securing areas in which wiring and cabling are located and those standards should be uniformly applied throughout your facility. Security procedures that need to be developed for wiring and cabling are shown Table 4.4. The checklist can be used by the physical IT security working group during their review of the drafted procedures to determine if all of the necessary areas have been covered.

Table 4.4   *Checklist for Wiring and Cabling Security Procedures*

Types of Procedures Needed	Status (completed, pending, not applicable)
How is access to wiring and cabling areas controlled and monitored?	Enter status for each area in this column.
What types of doors and locks are used to secure wiring and cabling areas?	

Table 4.4 *Checklist for Wiring and Cabling Security Procedures (continued)*

Types of Procedures Needed	Status (completed, pending, not applicable)
What types of alarms or monitoring systems are used for controlling access to wiring and cabling areas?	
Who can authorize access to wiring and cabling areas?	
How are service providers monitored when and if they need to access wiring and cabling areas?	
How are maintenance and access logs for wiring and cabling areas maintained?	
How are keys or key codes for the wiring and cabling areas managed and controlled?	
How are the signals transmitted over wiring and cabling protected from interception?	

4.7   Security Procedures for Remote Computers

Physical security procedures for remote computing devices, including mobile computing devices, are often overlooked. Remote computing can include any stationary device not located within your facility that connects to one of your computers. Mobile computing includes remote connected devices that are moved from location to location. For the purposes of physical security the type of device is far less important than the environment in which it is located and operated.

Because stationary devices can be connected, or logged on, to your systems, you should set the same type of physical security requirements for those devices as you do for those devices that are connected to your systems from within your facility. The major goal is to ensure that devices are not logged onto your system and left unattended, potentially allowing unauthorized users to gain access to your data and systems.

Mobile computing devices are also subject to loss or theft, which may make it easier for unauthorized persons to access your system. Loss or theft may also expose proprietary information to unauthorized viewers.

Security procedures that should be developed for remote and mobile computing devices are shown Table 4.5. The checklist can be used by the physical IT security working group to review the comprehensiveness of the drafted procedures.

Table 4.5 *Checklist for Remote and Mobile Device Security Procedures*

Types of Procedures Needed	Status (completed, pending, not applicable)
How are users automatically logged off the host system when it is not being used?	Enter status for each area in this column.
How are user profiles and passwords managed on remote computing devices?	
Note environmental and structural protection for remote computing devices.	
Note physical access controls for remote and mobile computing devices.	
Include property tags and other identification systems for mobile computing devices.	
How is used equipment disposed of and who is responsible for disposal?	

4.8   Security Procedures for Desktops

Desktop computers pose several types of security problems. The physical IT security working group needs to be concerned with keeping unauthorized persons from removing, moving, opening, or tampering with desktop computers. The placement of desktop devices also needs to be considered to prevent unauthorized persons from viewing the content displayed on monitors.

Security procedures that need to be developed for desktops computing devices are shown Table 4.6. The checklist can be used by the physical IT security working group during their review of the drafted procedures to ensure that all needs are being met.

Table 4.6 *Checklist for Desktop Computing Devices Security Procedures*

Types of Procedures Needed	Status (completed, pending, not applicable)
Secure placement and protection of equipment within offices or other work areas.	Enter status for each area in this column.
Provide protection for cabling, plugs, and other wires that connect the devices to your network.	

Table 4.6   *Checklist for Desktop Computing Devices Security Procedures (continued)*

Types of Procedures Needed	Status (completed, pending, not applicable)
How are users automatically logged off the host system when it is not being used?	
List environmental and structural protection measures for desktop computing devices.	
Include property tags and other identification systems for desktop computing devices.	
Note security for computer cases to deter unauthorized entry into systems as well as removal or installation of items such as memory, boards, ports, etc.	
List theft deterrent procedures, which may include lockdown.	
How are desktop computers protected from electrical surges or power outages?	
How is used equipment disposed of and who is responsible for disposal?	

4.9   Security Procedures for Department-Based Servers

Procedures to protect department-based servers are similar to those for desktop computers and remote computing devices. Security procedures that need to be developed for department-based servers are shown Table 4.7. The checklist can be used by the physical IT security working group to ensure that adequate procedures have been developed.

Table 4.7   *Checklist for Department-Based Servers Security Procedures*

Types of Procedures Needed	Status (completed, pending, not applicable)
How are server areas protected in offices or other work areas?	Enter status for each area in this column.
Provide protection for cabling, plugs, and other wires that connect the devices to your network or connect the servers to local devices.	

Table 4.7   *Checklist for Department-Based Servers Security Procedures (continued)*

Types of Procedures Needed	Status (completed, pending, not applicable)
Use property tags and other identification systems for department-based servers.	
Provide security for department-based server cases to deter unauthorized entry into systems as well as removal or installation of items such as memory, boards, ports, etc.	
List theft deterrent procedures, which may include lockdown or enclosure security.	
How are department-based servers protected from electrical surges or power outages?	
How is used equipment disposed of and who is responsible for disposal?	

4.10   Security Procedures for Telecom and Datacom Equipment

Telcom and datacom equipment includes switches, routers, hubs, telephones, PBXs, voicemail systems, and printer sharing equipment, regardless of where the equipment is located. The most expensive equipment is probably located in or near the data center. However, depending on when and how networks were installed, there could very well be a wide variety of devices spread through your offices, warehouses, or manufacturing areas.

Table 4.8 shows security procedures that need to be developed for telecom and datacom equipment. The checklist is designed to help the physical IT working group review drafted procedures to make sure all issues have been addressed.

Table 4.8   *Checklist for Telecom and Datacom Equipment Security Procedures*

Types of Procedures Needed	Status (completed, pending, not applicable)
Provide secure placement and protection of equipment within offices, other work areas, wiring and cabling areas, and in the data center.	Enter status for each area in this column.

Table 4.8 *Checklist for Telecom and Datacom Equipment Security Procedures (continued)*

Types of Procedures Needed	Status (completed, pending, not applicable)
Use property tags and other identification systems for telecom and datacom equipment.	
List types of doors and locks used to secure telecom and datacom equipment areas as well as the types of racks or mounting devices that should be used to install the equipment.	
What types of alarms or monitoring systems are used for controlling access to telecom and datacom equipment?	
Who can authorize access to telecom and datacom equipment areas?	
How are service providers monitored when and if they need to access telecom and datacom equipment areas?	
How are maintenance and access for telecom and datacom equipment maintained?	
How are keys or key codes for telecom and datacom equipment areas managed and controlled?	
How and when are voice system user logs reviewed and how are reports of misuse handled?	
How is used telecom and datacom equipment disposed of and who is responsible for disposal?	

4.11 Security Procedures for Manufacturing Control Equipment

If your organization is involved in manufacturing, then it is likely that you have some type of electrical or electronic manufacturing control equipment. During the last two decades much of this equipment has been computerized or is controlled or monitored using software that runs on desktop computers or servers. Security of this equipment is as important as it is for business types of computing devices and networks. Many of the same physical security methods and procedures can be applied to manufacturing control equipment. As with other areas, a checklist of security procedures that need to be developed for manufacturing control equipment is shown Table 4.9.

Table 4.9   *Checklist for Manufacturing Control Equipment Security Procedures*

Types of Procedures Needed	Status (completed, pending, not applicable)
Provide secure placement and protection of equipment within other work areas, including cabinetry, rack mounting, and relative location to other types of equipment.	Enter status for each area in this column.
Provide protection for cabling, plugs, and other wires that connect the devices to your network or to automated manufacturing equipment.	
Use property tags and other identification systems for manufacturing control equipment.	
List the types of alarms or monitoring systems used for controlling access to manufacturing control equipment.	
How are service providers monitored when and if they need to work on manufacturing control equipment?	
How are maintenance and access logs for manufacturing control equipment maintained?	
How is used manufacturing control equipment disposed of and who is responsible for disposal?	

4.12 Security Procedures for Surveillance and Alarm Systems

Most smaller organizations do not have much in the way of surveillance and alarm systems. However, the majority of large organizations have surveillance and alarm systems of some type installed. These systems are of little use if they can be readily accessed and disabled. In addition, many new versions of surveillance and alarm systems have been computerized and are controlled by software that runs on desktop computers or smaller servers. Thus, it is advisable to develop appropriate physical security procedures for your surveillance and alarm systems. The procedures should be consistent with those developed for other types of IT equipment.

Physical security procedures for surveillance and alarm systems are similar in most ways to those for manufacturing control equipment and telecom and datacom equipment. Security procedures that need to be developed for surveillance and alarm systems are shown Table 4.10. The checklist can be used by the physical IT security working group to assure that procedures are comprehensive.

Table 4.10   *Checklist for Surveillance and Alarm System Security Procedures*

Types of Procedures Needed	Status (completed, pending, not applicable)
Provide secure placement and protection of surveillance and alarm systems within offices, other work areas, lobbies, and exterior areas of the buildings.	Enter status for each area in this column.
Provide protection for cabling, plugs, and other wires that connect the surveillance and alarm systems to your network or to outside networks used to notify emergency service providers.	
Use property tags and other identification systems for surveillance and alarm systems.	
List the types of doors and locks used to secure surveillance and alarm system areas.	
Who can authorize access to surveillance and alarm system areas and how are maintenance and access logs for surveillance and alarm systems maintained?	
How are service providers monitored when and if they need to access surveillance and alarm systems?	
How are keys or key codes surveillance and alarm system areas managed and controlled?	
How is used surveillance and alarm equipment disposed of and who is responsible for disposal?	

4.13   Action Steps to Improve Physical IT Security

The material in this chapter shows the major elements of a physical IT security plan and recommends a structure for the documentation of the plan and accompanying procedures. As steps are taken to improve physical security of

IT assets, managers, planners, and technical staff should understand the following principles:

- Physical IT security plans and procedures should be easy to read and understand.

- The documentation for plans and procedures should be compiled, written, or assembled following the quality control recommendations in this chapter.

- Plans and procedures should cover the entire range of computing devices used by your organization as well as those that access your systems remotely.

There are several steps that organizations can take to help improve the physical security of IT assets. Recommended steps are included at the end of each chapter. The action steps listed in Table 4.11 are designed to help organize and structure the development of a physical IT security plan.

Table 4.11   *Action Steps to Improve Physical IT Security*

Step Number	Action Step
4.01	Identify which areas (from those listed in this chapter) need to have physical IT security policies and procedures developed for them.
4.02	Develop a tentative list of procedures that need to be developed for each of the areas you identified as needing physical security procedures.
4.03	Review the practices in Chapter 1 that are recommended to counter various types of and select those that best meet the needs of your organization.
4.04	Assign members of the working group the responsibility for drafting procedures for those areas that you have determined need procedures.
4.05	Convene the physical IT working group and review the status of work on developing the tentative list of needed procedures and prepare to move ahead with developing draft procedures.

5

Developing and Documenting Methods and Procedures

At this point you should have identified the areas for which you need to develop physical IT security policies and procedures (as discussed in Chapter 4). The areas for which you may need procedures include: data centers, wiring and cabling, remote computing devices, desktop computers, department-based servers, telecom and datacom equipment, manufacturing control equipment, and surveillance and alarm systems. You also should have determined how responsibilities for physical IT security will be spread across the various departments in your organization.

The physical IT working group should have developed a tentative list of procedures that need to be developed for each of the areas you identified as needing physical security procedures. The action steps in Chapter 3 called for evaluations of existing risk exposure: cyber security, disaster recovery, and business continuity plans; legal and regulatory requirements; and insurance requirements and opportunities to reduce insurance premium cost. The results of these evaluations will help the working group develop the list of needed procedures.

In addition, you should have determined how administrative support will be provided to the working group in their efforts to create the documents that communicate what the procedures are and who has responsibility for those procedures.

If you have performed all of the recommended action steps and assembled all of this material you are now ready to develop and document procedures. Table 5.1 shows the various lists of procedures the working group should have compiled.

Table 5.1 *Checklist for Material Needed to Start Developing Procedures*

Types of Procedures Needed	Status (completed, pending, not applicable)
List of procedures needed to support disaster recovery plans	Enter status for each area in this column.
List of procedures needed to support business continuity plans	
List of procedures needed to support cyber security plans	
List of procedures needed to be in compliance with laws and regulations	
List of procedures needed to be in compliance with insurance policy requirements	
List of procedures needed to obtain reduced insurance premiums	
List of selected practices from Chapter 1	
List of needed procedures from checklists in Chapter 4	

5.1   The Process of Developing Methods and Procedures

Developing and documenting procedures requires a sense of balance. You need to determine what is worth documenting. There is also a distinctive difference between standards and procedures. One rule of thumb is to create procedures only for those things that need to be performed by people on a repeated basis.

When you examine the materials you have assembled in preparation for developing and documenting physical IT security procedures, you can save time and effort by standing back and examining what you need to do once and what you need to repeat over and over again.

A good example is examining what kind of doors you want to install for wiring and cabling areas or equipment rooms. The most commonly recommended door and lock system is a steel frame with a steel door that has a heavy-duty deadbolt type of lock. You install the door and the lock once and you have met a great standard and implemented a widely recognized security practice. However, it does not necessarily need to be documented as a procedure.

On the other hand, how access is controlled and who authorizes access to the wiring and cabling or equipment rooms is something that will have to be repeated over and over again. This should be documented as a procedure.

There are several basic steps to developing procedures for physical security. These steps will differ slightly from area to area, depending on the complexity of the procedures and the departments responsible for implementing the procedures. The basic steps are:

1.   Identify the needed procedures.

2.   Group related procedures.

3.   Draft the procedure in accordance with external requirements (i.e., disaster recovery plans or laws and regulations).

4.   Have the working group review each procedure.

5.   Modify each procedure based on input from the working group.

6.   Have employees who are responsible for executing the procedure read and walk through execution.

7.   Modify the procedure based on input from the testing employee.

8.   Copyedit and proofread the procedure.

9.   Finalize the format of the procedure and document accordingly.

5.2   Devising a Format for Documenting Procedures

The next thing you need to decide on is a uniform format for documenting procedures. The working group on physical IT security should review how procedures are documented in the cyber security and disaster recovery plan as well as other procedure manuals that your organization maintains. It is possible that one of the existing procedure formats will be adequate to support this documentation effort. Figure 5.1 shows a basic procedure format.

Explanations of the fields in the procedure format are as follows:

■   The procedure name should be straightforward and describe what the procedure governs.

■   The procedure numbers should be grouped according to the purpose of the procedure. For example, data center access procedures could all be numbered 1100 through 1199.

Figure 5.1

Sample Procedure Format

Procedure name	Procedure number
Purpose of the procedure	
Responsible departments	
Details of the procedure	
Plans or policies procedure supports	Date of last revision
Page x of x	

- The purpose of the procedure should briefly state why the procedure was developed and the objective that is met by the procedure.

- The responsible departments field should indicate all of the departments that have any responsibility for implementing the procedure. Details of responsibility can be indicated in the details field.

- The details of the procedure field indicate the steps that staff should take to meet the requirements of the procedure.

- The plans or policies supported field should indicate whether the procedure was designed to help support cyber security, disaster recovery, or meet the requirements of a specified law or regulation.

- The date of last revision field should show just that.

5.3   Physical Security Procedures for Data Centers

As with all areas for which procedures are developed, physical IT security procedures for data centers should support related plans including cyber security, disaster recovery, or business continuity, or help comply with related laws and regulations. In addition to the steps outlined in the preceding section for developing procedures, there are several things to keep in mind when developing procedures specifically for data centers.

- Data center security procedures may be considerably more complex than those for other areas such as wiring and cabling located outside the data center.

- Data center security procedures usually contain technical terminology that needs to be checked for accuracy.

- It may be more expedient to include physical security procedures for data centers as a subsection of a data center procedures manual rather than creating a separate stand-alone document.

- As data center security procedures are being developed it is advisable to have a variety of people within the data center review the procedures. Select staff who will be affected by a procedure because of their particular work areas or types of expertise.

- You should not assume that because the data center has access control, extra levels of security are not necessary for sensitive documents or critical types of equipment within the data center.

5.4 Physical Security Procedures for Wiring and Cabling

It is likely that many types of employees will need to be briefed or fully trained on wiring and cabling security procedures. This could include the building maintenance staff because they have responsibility for the physical upkeep of the facility and will be accessing much of the building at one time or another. The janitorial service and cleaning staff may very well have a similar scope of responsibility. If these employees do not understand the requirements for securing wiring and cabling areas then they could very well inadvertently cause a security breach.

In addition to the steps designed for developing procedures, there are several things to keep in mind when developing procedures specifically for wiring and cabling.

- Procedures that require action on the part of building maintenance or janitorial staff should be written in a very straightforward manner.

- Because of the diverse audience that needs to understand the physical security procedures for wiring and cabling areas the procedures should be as jargon-free as possible.

- The procedures included in manuals that are used by security staff or referred to by supervisors of building maintenance and janitorial staff, as well as other employees outside of the network design or management staff, should not include diagrams of buildings or detailed explanations of network design.

5.5   Physical Security Procedures for Remote Computers

Physical security procedures for remote computers may need to be developed for multiple audiences. This could include the IT staff at the offices of your customers or suppliers that you allow to access your systems. It could also include sales people who spend much of their time in the field, and middle managers who use laptops to access your business computers.

In addition to the guidelines for developing procedures, there are several things to keep in mind when developing procedures specifically for remote computers.

- Specific procedures should be developed for the different types of remote or mobile computing devices that are used to access your systems.

- Physical security procedures for laptop computers that are used by different types of employees should specifically address the types of environments from which they connect to your systems (i.e., hotels, airports, and customer offices).

- Procedures that are distributed to remote uses should not include information about the security technologies or methods employed to protect your systems—they should just describe the behavioral steps you want remote users to perform.

- Procedures for remote users should include a phone number as well as an e-mail address of contacts from whom they can obtain assistance or of whom they can ask questions about the procedures.

5.6   Physical Security Procedures for Desktops

Physical security procedures for desktop computers also should be directed at several audiences. Individual users need to know their responsibilities for the physical security of the computers they use. Procedures should be developed that address the role of department managers and supervisors in enforcing procedures and monitoring the compliance of individual computer-using employees. The IT staff who maintain desktop computers should also play a role in ensuring that end-users are complying with procedures.

In addition to the steps outlined for developing procedures, there are several things to keep in mind when developing procedures specifically for desktop computing devices.

- Because of the diverse audience that needs to understand the physical security procedures for desktop computers, the procedures should be as jargon-free as possible.

- Procedures that are distributed to desktop users should not include information about the security technologies or methods employed to protect your systems—they should just describe the behavioral steps that you want desktop users to perform.

- All procedures for desktop security should describe the responsibilities of individual employees as well as their supervisors and department managers.

- If more than one type of desktop is used in the organization and if the various machines require different procedures, you should identify which type of machine a procedure is designed to protect.

- Desktop procedures should cover all of the peripherals used throughout the organization.

- Security procedures for desktop computers should cover the security of magnetic media used by the employees as well as the documents employees print from their computers.

5.7   Physical Security Procedures for Department-Based Servers

Physical security procedures for department-based servers also should be directed at several audiences. Procedures should be developed that address the role of department managers and supervisors in enforcing procedures and monitoring the compliance of employees in their departments. The IT staff who maintain department-based servers should also play a role in ensuring that departmental personnel are complying with procedures.

In addition to the steps outlined for developing procedures, there are several things to keep in mind when developing procedures specifically for department-based servers.

- Procedures that are distributed to departments where servers are located should not include information about the security technologies or methods employed to protect your systems—they should just describe the behavioral steps you want department personnel to perform.

- If there is more than one type of server and if security procedures differ for the various types of servers, procedures should be developed for each type of server.

- All procedures for department-based server security should describe the responsibilities of individual employees as well as their supervisors and department managers.

- Desktop procedures should cover all of the peripherals attached to servers.

- Security procedures for servers should cover the devices that connect the server to the main network as well as to local machines.

- Security procedures for servers should cover the security of backup tapes.

5.8   Physical Security Procedures for Telecom and Datacom Equipment

Physical security procedures for telecom and datacom equipment should be developed for each type of equipment and for the various environments in which the equipment is located. This is especially true for voice communications devices. Individual users need to know their responsibilities for the physical security of their voice units. Procedures also should be developed that address the role of department managers and supervisors in enforcing procedures and monitoring the compliance of individual employees. The telecom staff who maintain voice devices also should play a role in ensuring that end users are complying with procedures.

If routers or hubs are located throughout the building, then procedures need to be developed that address the role of department managers and supervisors in enforcing procedures for equipment located in their work areas. The network management staff that maintains the various networking devices also should play a role in ensuring that employees where equipment is located are complying with procedures.

In addition to the steps outlined for developing procedures, there are several things to keep in mind when developing procedures specifically for telecom and datacom equipment.

- Procedures for distributed telecom and datacom equipment should cover access control.

- Procedures that are distributed to departments where telecom and datacom equipment are located should not include information about the security technologies or methods employed to protect your systems—they should just describe the behavioral steps that you want department personnel to perform.

- Because of the diverse audience that needs to understand the physical security procedures for telecom and datacom equipment that is located through the facility, procedures should be as jargon-free as possible.

- Procedures for distributed telecom and datacom equipment should address the roles of individual employees, supervisors, and department managers.

- Procedures should cover the installation and de-installation of voice equipment and explain who is authorized to perform those duties.

- All employees should be trained on security procedures for voice equipment.

5.9 Physical Security Procedures for Manufacturing Control Equipment

It is likely that many types of employees will need to be briefed or fully trained on security procedures for manufacturing control equipment. This could include the building maintenance staff because they have responsibility for the physical upkeep of the areas where this equipment is located. The same applies to janitorial service and cleaning staff who may be cleaning in areas where the equipment is located. It will certainly include all of the users of the equipment and their supervisors.

Procedures also need to address responsibilities of department managers and supervisors who work in manufacturing areas. They will have some responsibility for ensuring that individual employees comply with security procedures for the manufacturing control systems in the areas in which they work. In addition to the steps outlined for developing procedures, there are several things to keep in mind when developing procedures specifically for manufacturing control equipment.

- Security procedures for manufacturing control equipment should cover all of the backup tapes and disks used for the systems.

- Procedures should cover the operation manuals for all of the manufacturing control equipment.

- Procedures should cover the security of configuration information and settings for all manufacturing control equipment.

- Procedures should cover who is authorized to install, modify, and configure manufacturing control equipment.

- Procedures that are distributed to manufacturing personnel should not include information about the security technologies or methods employed to protect your systems—they should just describe the behavioral steps you want department personnel to perform.

- Because of the diverse audience that needs to understand the physical security procedures for manufacturing control systems the procedures should be as jargon-free as possible.

5.10 Physical Security Procedures for Surveillance and Alarm Systems

Procedures for the physical security of surveillance and alarm systems will need to be developed to address the responsibilities of a variety of employees. As with other types of equipment that are located throughout the facility, this could include the building maintenance staff because they have responsibility for the physical upkeep of the areas where this equipment is located. The same applies to janitorial service and cleaning staff who may be cleaning in areas where the equipment is located.

Procedures also need to address responsibilities of department managers and supervisors who work in any area where surveillance and alarm systems are located. They will have some responsibility for ensuring that individual employees comply with security procedures for systems in the areas in which they work.

In addition to the steps outlined for developing procedures, there are several things to keep in mind when developing procedures specifically for surveillance and alarm systems.

- Security procedures for surveillance and alarm systems should not include any information on how the systems work.

- Procedures for surveillance and alarm systems should cover all of the documents pertaining to configuration and operation of the equipment.

- Procedures should not reveal the locations of sensors of monitoring devices to persons who do not have a specific need to know.

- Procedures should specify who is authorized to work on surveillance and alarm systems.

- Procedures should not provide details on how surveillance and alarm systems are connected to internal or external networks.

5.11 Action Steps to Improve Physical IT Security

The material in this chapter shows how to develop and document physical IT security procedures. As steps are taken to improve physical security of IT assets, managers, planners, and technical staff should understand the following concepts:

- Procedures should be developed for data centers, wiring and cabling, remote computing devices, desktop computers, department-based servers, telecom and datacom equipment, manufacturing control equipment, and surveillance and alarm systems

- Procedures should be developed to support cyber security, disaster recovery, and business continuity plans.

- Procedures should be developed to meet insurance requirements and obtain discounts on insurance premiums when possible.

- Procedures should be developed to meet the requirements of laws and regulations that govern your business sector.

- Procedures should be developed using a structured approach for drafting, reviewing, and finalizing the procedure.

- There are several differences in the audiences that must understand physical security procedures, many of which will not have a sophisticated IT background.

There are several steps that organizations can take to help improve the physical security of IT assets. Recommended steps are included at the end of each chapter. The action steps listed in Table 5.2 are designed to help an organization develop and document physical IT security procedures.

Table 5.2   *Action Steps to Improve Physical IT Security*

Step Number	Action Step
5.01	Assemble the checklists from Chapter 4 that show what physical IT security procedures should cover for each area and the list of procedures that the working group decided should be developed. Use those lists to prioritize procedure development.
5.02	Devise a uniform format for documenting procedures.
5.03	Draft and test needed procedures.
5.04	Finalize the procedures and create documentation.
5.05	Using the list of procedures that the working group decided were necessary procedures, check that they have been developed and are included in the documentation.

6

Auditing and Testing Procedures

Security needs to be an ongoing concern. You should not fall into complacency once your physical IT security plan and procedures are documented and your employees have been trained. Maintaining security procedures is a constant and continuous process. This process can be simplified by employing three techniques: auditing compliance with procedures; periodically testing procedures and groups of related procedures; and training IT, security staff, department supervisors and managers to embed ongoing monitoring and reporting practices in their daily routines.

The process of developing procedures described in Chapter 5 is designed to help you quickly develop and document a wide variety of physical IT security procedures. However, to ensure that your procedures can be effective over a long period, it is advisable to audit and test those procedures on a regular basis. This process will help you adjust procedures when the physical layout of offices or facilities is modified, when new equipment is installed, or when new and improved security systems are installed. This chapter presents auditing and testing techniques designed to help keep your physical IT procedures current and effective.

6.1   How to Audit and Test Procedures

There are several steps that should be followed to audit and test physical IT security procedures. The auditing process involves reviewing procedures to ensure that they are current and monitoring compliance with procedures. Neither of these methods is complex. They do, however, require time and attention to detail.

Auditing procedures to make sure they are current primarily involves reviewing and examining procedures to identify any reason that they may not work. Staff that have been working in the ongoing management of IT operations, organization security, or equipment installation can contribute to the examination. The advantage of assigning personnel with this level of involvement is that they have knowledge about what may have changed.

Another approach to the auditing process is to examine compliance with documented procedures. This is relatively easy to do in situations in which a condition is supposed to exist. Keeping doors to all wiring closets locked when there are no authorized personnel present, for example, is a condition: the doors should be locked. The storage of sensitive material is another example. Procedures usually call for sensitive material to be secured when it is not in use by authorized personnel.

Auditing compliance with procedures should be done on a periodic and unannounced basis. An IT manager or security manager should walk through facilities with a checklist of conditions that should exist. The manager should identify and note any situation in which procedurally required conditions are not met. Immediately after the audit the manager should report situations that need to be rectified. Table 6.1 shows a sample checklist for auditing compliance with security procedures that require areas to be locked.

Once the identified security problems are rectified, security managers need to examine the identified security problems, analyze trends they reveal, and determine who is responsible for violating the procedures. It is important to note that what is being analyzed is trends. Prior to taking any disciplinary action against individual employees, it is wise to determine why a condition exists or a procedure was not properly executed. Although there are situations in which disciplinary action may be warranted, it is best to deal with less significant violations through additional training.

Table 6.1   *Checklist for Auditing Compliance with Security Procedures*

List of conditions to comply with procedures	Status (compliant, uncertain, not compliant)
Lock second-floor wiring closet door.	Enter status for each area in this column.
Lock server room located in accounting department.	
Lock telcom closet located in the business office.	
Lock network equipment room in the data center.	
Lock surveillance equipment closet in lobby.	
Lock media room in data center.	
Lock cabinets with on-site backup tapes.	

The third method to determine how well physical IT security procedures are working, or can be executed, is to create a test scenario that requires staff to respond to a simulated situation. The emergency evacuation of a data center, for example, is an excellent test to determine if the IT staff can respond quickly and perform basic tasks necessary to ensure that all security procedures have been implemented as they leave the data center.

It is also advisable to train employees to routinely observe whether physical IT security procedures are being followed. Once IT and security staff understand what the procedures are, they can observe compliance with those procedures on a daily basis. They should also report problems that they observe. Figure 6.1 shows a sample physical IT security procedure violation report.

Explanations of the fields in the procedure violation report form are as follows:

- The date field should show the date that the violation occurred or was discovered.

- The reporting employee field should show the name of the employee who discovered the violation.

Figure 6.1

Sample Procedure Violation Report

Date	Reporting Employee
Procedure name	Procedure number
Who violated the procedure (if known)	
Reason for the violation (if known)	
Details of the violation	
Training status of the violator (if known)	Date of last revision of the procedure
Page x of x	

- The procedure name should be straightforward and descriptive of what the procedure governs and should come from the procedure manual.

- The procedure numbers should come from the procedure manual.

- The field labeled "Who violated the procedure (if known)" should indicate the name or names of the individual(s) who violated the procedure.

- The field labeled "Reason for the violation (if known)" should note why the violation occurred. This could include a lack of training or knowledge on the part of an untrained employee or a recent change in a procedure that was not communicated to employees.

- The details of the violation field indicate what condition or activity was compliant with procedures.

- The field for the "training status of the violator (if known)" should indicate the last date of any training the employee may have had about physical IT procedures.

- The field for the date of last revision of the procedure should show just that.

6.2   Auditing and Testing for Data Centers

All of the methods mentioned in the preceding section can be used to audit and test compliance with procedures in a data center. However, each method needs to be tailored to the physical IT security procedures that have been developed for the data center.

To effectively employ the audit process using staff to review procedures for relevance and currency, a project manager should be designated to assign reviews to appropriate staff. The project manager should assign specific procedures for staff review on a regular basis. It is advisable to assign reviews in relatively small batches so that IT staff can perform the reviews during the course of a one-week period.

The reviews can be done on paper copies or electronic copies. The staff performing the reviews should approve the procedure as it is written or they can recommend changes. If changes are recommended, the staff person should provide a brief description of why a change should be made and how it should be made.

The recommended changes should be reviewed by security supervisors or other data center managers who may be affected by the changes. If the changes are found to be acceptable, then a new procedure should be drafted. The draft procedure should be reviewed just as if it was a newly formulated procedure by using the procedure development process provided in Chapter 5.

This review process can be used for other major areas discussed in this chapter, including desktop computers and department-based servers. Each subsection of this chapter indicates which auditing and testing methods are best for a different type of equipment and its security needs and how to tailor those methods to the procedures that are specific to each area.

It is also possible to develop compliance checklists that can be used to audit compliance with physical IT security procedures for the data center. Several types of checklists are helpful, including those to audit compliance with procedures for:

- Securing entrances and exits to the data center

- Securing sensitive documents within the data center

- Disposing of used media and printed material produced by the data center

- Allowing access of visitors and service personnel

- Maintaining environmental control of the data center, including air conditioning; heating, moisture, and temperature control; and fire suppression systems

- Maintaining service logs for data center equipment

- Protecting lists of user names, passwords, and other system access control procedures and processes

- Protecting information relating to security settings on systems

The checklists should be used on a periodic basis to audit compliance with physical IT security procedures for the data center. When violations of procedures are discovered, training sessions should be developed for IT staff and supervisors to present the violations that were found. The checklists should be used again within 60 days to determine if the training was effective.

It is also advisable for data center supervisors to embed compliance monitoring in their daily routines. By doing so, security violations can be discovered as they occur and individual employees can be counseled on their compliance with the procedures. It is important to note that supervisors and managers who work in the data center should set an example by constantly complying with the physical IT security procedures.

It is also advisable to develop tests of related procedures and have drills to determine if data center personnel respond appropriately. One drill to consider is to test whether data center staff can properly handle a suspicious package. Figure 6.2 shows a sample procedure for identifying suspicious packages that was developed based on the Centers for Disease Control and Prevention's FAQs regarding anthrax (www.bt.cdc.gov). You can conduct training on the procedure and then develop a drill to see how staff respond.

Figure 6.2

Sample Procedures for Identifying Suspicious Packages

Procedures for Identifying Suspicious Packages	Procedure number: Data Center 1201
Purpose of the procedure is to guide data center personnel in dealing with involving suspicious letters, packages or containers.	
Responsible departments: Shipping and receiving, mailroom, data center staff that process incoming packages.	

All packages should be examined before they are opened and the following items checked:

- The package is addressed to a person that does not work in the data center nor has ever worked in the data center.

- The package has excessive postage adhered to it.

- The address is handwritten or poorly typed.

- Package has many misspellings of common words.

- There is a strange, unknown, or no return address.

- The package is marked with restrictions such as "Personal," "Confidential" or "Do not x-ray."

- The package is marked with any threatening language.

- A powdery substance be felt through or appearing on the package.

- Package has oily stains, discolorations or odor.

- There is excessive packaging material such as masking tape, string, etc.

- The package is excessively heavy.

- There is a ticking sound, protruding wires, or aluminum foil.

- Other suspicious signs.

If a package or envelope appears suspicious:	
• Staff should notify a supervisor and security.	
• All non emergency personnel should leave the area.	
• Law enforcement agency should be called.	
• Ideally, only those with hazardous material training should proceed to handle the package when necessary.	
Supports corporate security plan and disaster recovery plan	Date of last revision: December 1, 2004
Page 1 of 1	

Figure 6.2 *(continued)*

6.3   Auditing and Testing Wiring and Cabling Security

Auditing compliance with physical IT procedures for wiring and cabling security is relatively straightforward compared to data centers. The best methods to test compliance with procedures for the security of wiring and cabling are periodic audits using checklists and embedded monitoring. Walkthroughs with checklists are advisable on a periodic basis, but embedded monitoring will be the most effective approach.

If your organization has security personnel who patrol your facilities they should routinely check to make sure that wiring and cabling closets are locked. Network management staff also should make checks when they go to a particular wiring and cabling closet to perform work. If security personnel or network management staff discover violations of procedures they should file violation reports.

In addition to monitoring the security of wiring and cabling closets, it is important to recognize that people like to fill up what they think are empty spaces. You should routinely check to make sure that wiring and cabling closets do not become storage lockers for empty boxes and obsolete computer equipment. A checklist similar to the one presented in Figure 6.1 can be used for a periodic inspection.

A more complicated concern about wiring and cabling security ensuring that physical IT security procedures for cabling that connects desktop computers, department-based servers, manufacturing control systems, and surveillance and alarm systems remain secure. Such checks can be included when auditing compliance with physical IT security procedures for those types of equipment.

6.4   Auditing and Testing Remote Computer Procedures

The best method to test compliance with procedures by remote computer users is embedded monitoring. This includes evaluating help desk requests from remote or mobile users. It is also helpful to analyze the access log entries created by remote users.

Monitoring compliance for mobile computer users is difficult because they often spend more time in the field and there is less opportunity to observe their behavior. However, it is helpful to use the help desk function to identify potential compromises and to examine the access log entries created by mobile computing devices.

Methods allowing the help desk to monitor compliance with physical IT procedures for remote and mobile computing can also be transformed into an enforcement and prevention effort. The help desk staff should monitor behaviors of users that could be indications that the remote or mobile computer has been compromised and an unauthorized person is attempting to access your systems, including the following:

- Repeated call from the same user with log in problems

- Calls from a user who states that he or she has an emergency and has lost the necessary password

- Calls from a user asking questions about accessing system functions to which that user should not have access

- Calls from a person claiming to be the user's boss or replacement but who does not have any knowledge of how the system works

You should have developed procedures to address these potential situations. If you have not, the help desk should report a possible violation of physical IT security procedures for remote or mobile computing. In some cases the user's request will be legitimate, but you should recognize that such behaviors could in fact be indicative of a compromise. Above all, the help desk staff should be trained to be suspicious.

Another embedded approach to monitoring compliance with physical IT security procedures for remote and mobile computers is for the network management staff to examine login attempts from recognized systems. This examination can be made in a number of ways and can be automated to send alarms to security, network management staff, or the help desk.

In the event that a laptop or other mobile computing device is lost or stolen, the user of the device should immediately contact security or the help desk and report the incident. This way user names and passwords can be quickly disabled. But in an imperfect world, the user may not in fact know that the device was compromised. Thus good help desk practices can help to prevent unauthorized system access.

6.5 Auditing and Testing Desktop Procedures

Enforcing physical security procedures for desktop computers poses several challenges. Simply stated, most people do not take the security of desktop computers seriously. Most of the methods mentioned in the preceding section can be used to audit and test compliance with procedures for the security of desktop computers.

Developing a series of checklists for auditing compliance with procedures may be necessary and can include a checklist for business-hours security checks and after-hours security checks. The checklist can also cross over into some cyber security issues. The content of the checklists will of course depend on your procedures, but popular items include:

- Checking that users properly log off their systems during periods of nonuse or when they leave the office

- Checking that users have not moved their desktop computer to a less secure physical position

- Checking to see that passwords are not written on Post-It notes and stuck to the computer or other places in the work area

- Examining the desktop computer for unauthorized peripheral devices or wireless networking devices

- Checking the desktop computer to ensure that users have not installed unauthorized software

- Checking the desktop computer to determine if the user has changed configuration settings in a manner that will make the computer less secure

Embedded monitoring techniques can be employed when your desktop technicians visit offices to troubleshoot problems with desktops, upgrade systems with new components or software, or work on peripheral devices. Embedded monitoring can also be done by supervisors or managers for their surrounding work area.

Testing related procedures for desktop security can be accomplished through simple evacuation drills in which employees are supposed to shut down equipment and lock their offices as they leave.

6.6   Auditing and Testing Procedures for Department-Based Servers

Depending on the physical location of a department-based server, enforcing physical security procedures can be as challenging as it is for desktop computers. Again, most people do not take the security of department-based servers seriously. All of the methods mentioned in the preceding section can be used to audit and test compliance with procedures for the security of department-based servers.

As with desktop computers, developing a series of checklists for auditing compliance with department-based server security procedures may be necessary. There also may be some cross-over into some cyber security issues. The content of the checklists will of course depend on your procedures, but popular items include:

- If applicable, checking that doors are locked to server areas
- Checking that department staff have not moved the server to a less secure physical position
- If department personnel have administrative access to a server, checking to see that passwords are not written on PostIit notes and stuck to the computer or other places in the server area
- Checking to make sure that the server area has not been turned into a storage area for boxes or obsolete office equipment, books, or magazines
- Checking the server to determine if department personnel who do have access have not changed configuration settings in a manner that will make the computer less secure

Embedded monitoring techniques can also be employed when your server technicians visit offices to troubleshoot problems with the server, upgrade systems with new components or software, or work on peripheral devices.

Embedded monitoring also can be done by supervisors or managers for their surrounding work area.

Testing related procedures for server security may be more difficult and could be limited to ensuring that the server area is locked, if applicable, during simple evacuation drills in which employees are supposed to shut down equipment and lock their offices as they leave. In most cases department employees do not shut down servers.

6.7   Auditing and Testing Telecom and Datacom Equipment Security

The best methods to test compliance with procedures for the security of telecom and datacom equipment are periodic audits using checklists and embedded monitoring. Appropriate checklists should be developed both for telecom and datacom equipment that is centralized and equipment that is decentralized. Centralized equipment can include PBX systems, voicemail systems, and WAN connectivity devices. Decentralized equipment can include desktop telephones or devices that support LANs such as hubs or routers.

Security needs and the monitoring tools will vary, depending on the size of an organization. In large organizations this equipment could occupy a space similar to that of a small data center with several trained staff operating and maintaining the equipment. In small organizations the equipment could occupy the space required for a few servers.

Regardless of the size and the amount of equipment used by an organization, it is important to ensure that physical security procedures are followed. The content of the checklists will of course depend on your procedures, but popular items include:

- Check that procedures are followed for securing entrances and exits to a large telecommunications center or to smaller server rooms.

- Check that sensitive documents are properly secured within the telecommunications center.

- Check that used media and printed material produced by the telecom staff are properly disposed of or properly stored.

- Check that procedures for access of equipment areas by visitors and service personnel are properly enforced.

- Check that environmental control of the telecommunications equipment rooms including air conditioning, heating, moisture, and temperature control as well as fire suppression systems are in proper working order.

- Check that proper methods are used to protect information relating to security settings on systems.

- If applicable, check that doors are locked to decentralized telecom and datacom equipment areas.

- Check that department staff have not moved decentralized telcom or datacom equipment to a less secure physical position.

- If department personnel have administrative access to decentralized computer-based telecom equipment, check to see that passwords are not written on Post-It notes and stuck to the computer or other places in the server area.

- Check to make sure that decentralized telecomm and datacom equipment areas have not been turned into storage areas for boxes or obsolete office equipment, books, or magazines.

Embedded monitoring techniques can be employed when your telecom and datacom technicians visit offices where decentralized equipment is located when they need to troubleshoot problems, conduct routine maintenance, or install upgraded or new software. Embedded monitoring also can be done by supervisors or managers for their surrounding work area. Testing related procedures for large telecommunications centers can be done in the same manner as for data centers.

6.8   Auditing and Testing Manufacturing Control Equipment Security

Because of the nature of many manufacturing areas, ensuring that physical security procedures are followed for the protection of manufacturing control equipment is often difficult. Many modern manufacturing facilities that rely heavily on automation have the equivalent of small data centers in the factory areas. However, smaller facilities often have servers, computers, wiring and cabling, and telecom and datacom equipment spread throughout the manufacturing area. Security in the smaller facilities is often more difficult to maintain.

If a manufacturing area has the equivalent of a small data center, then auditing and testing of physical security procedures should be conducted just as they would for a business data center. In smaller manufacturing environments most of the control equipment will be distributed throughout the facility just as desktop computers, servers, and other IT assets are distributed throughout the offices of a small organization. Applicable methods for auditing and testing compliance with desktop computers, servers, wiring and cabling, and telecom and datacom security procedures should be used just as they are in office areas.

Embedded monitoring is also important in manufacturing areas. Desktop technicians, telecom and datacom technicians, local supervisors, and department managers who work in manufacturing areas should be tasked with embedded monitoring just as those who work in office areas are tasked.

6.9   Auditing and Testing in Surveillance and Alarm System Security

The best methods to test compliance with procedures for the security of surveillance and alarm system equipment will depend on the type of equipment used and the size of the facility in which it is used. Periodic audits using checklists and embedded monitoring will work in most small organizations. However, many large organizations have security control rooms that are the size of small data centers.

Regardless of the size of the organization and the amount of surveillance and alarm system equipment used by an organization, it is important to ensure that physical security procedures are followed. As with telecom and datacom equipment, the content of the checklists will of course depend on your procedures, but popular items include:

- Check that procedures are followed for securing entrances and exits to surveillance and alarm system control centers.

- Check that sensitive documents are properly secured within the surveillance and alarm system control center.

- Check that used media and printed material produced by the security staff are properly disposed of or properly stored.

- Check that procedures for visitors and service personnel access of surveillance and alarm system equipment areas are properly enforced.

- Check that environmental control of the surveillance and alarm system control center and other equipment rooms including air conditioning, heating, moisture, and temperature control as well as fire suppression systems are in proper working order.

■ Check that proper methods are used to protect information relating to security settings on systems.

■ If applicable, check that doors are locked to decentralized surveillance and alarm system equipment areas.

■ Check that department staff have not moved decentralized surveillance and alarm system equipment in a manner that makes it less effective.

Embedded monitoring techniques also can be employed when your surveillance and alarm system technicians visit offices where decentralized equipment is located as they troubleshoot problems, conduct routine maintenance, or install upgrades. Embedded monitoring can be done by supervisors or managers for their surrounding work area. Testing related procedures for large surveillance and alarm system control center can be done in the same manner as for data centers.

6.10   Action Steps to Improve Physical IT Security

The material in this chapter shows how to audit and test physical IT security procedures. As steps are taken to improve physical security of IT assets, managers, planners, and technical staff should understand the following basic concepts:

■ Physical IT security procedures should be periodically reviewed to ensure that they are still applicable and effective.

■ There are several methods for conducting periodic reviews of physical IT security procedures, including auditing for currency and relevance, auditing for compliance, and testing the execution of related procedures.

■ Embed monitoring of security violations and the reporting of violations by observing employees.

There are several steps that organizations can take to help improve the physical security of IT assets. Recommended steps are included at the end of each chapter. The action steps listed in Table 6.2 are designed to help an organization design processes to audit and test physical IT security procedures.

Table 6.2 *Action Steps to Improve Physical IT Security*

Step Number	Action Step
6.01	Develop a set of checklists to audit physical IT security procedures.
6.02	Devise test process to test related physical IT security procedures such as an emergency evacuation of the data center.
6.03	Establish a tentative schedule for auditing and testing physical IT security procedures.
6.04	Develop an embedded monitoring and security violation reporting process for your organization.
6.05	Assign a subgroup of the physical IT working group to develop appropriate methods to audit and test compliance with procedures in a data center.
6.06	Assign a subgroup of the physical IT working group to develop appropriate methods to test adherence to security procedures for wiring and cabling.
6.07	Assign a subgroup of the physical IT working group to develop appropriate methods to test adherence to security procedures for remote computing.
6.08	Assign a subgroup of the physical IT working group to develop appropriate methods to test adherence to security procedures for desktop computers.
6.09	Assign a subgroup of the physical IT working group to develop appropriate methods to test adherence to security procedures for department-based servers.
6.10	Assign a subgroup of the physical IT working group to develop appropriate methods to test adherence to security procedures for telecom and datacom equipment.
6.11	Assign a subgroup of the physical IT working group to develop appropriate methods to test adherence to security procedures for manufacturing control equipment.
6.12	Assign a subgroup of the physical IT working group to develop appropriate methods to test adherence to security procedures for surveillance and alarm systems.
6.13	Convene the working group and review the methods developed by the subgroups for their assigned areas.

Table 6.2 *Action Steps to Improve Physical IT Security (continued)*

Step Number	Action Step
6.14	Conduct a test of all of the checklists the subgroups devised for auditing compliance with security procedures in their assigned areas.
6.15	Based on the experience of the working group, revise the checklist for auditing compliance with physical IT security procedures.
6.16	Assign a subgroup to devise a security violation reporting form and procedure.
6.17	Convene the working group to review the security violation reporting form and develop a recommendation to management for the adoption of the form and the reporting procedure.

7

The Role of the Incident Response Team

No matter how much effort you put forth to increase security awareness and to reduce risks, it is likely that at some time you will experience a physical IT security incident. This incident could result in a loss of data confidentiality, loss of data or system integrity, or disruption of availability. Because of this likelihood, organizations need a team that can respond to the physical IT security requirements and that team should be in place and know what they are going to do before an incident occurs.

The physical IT security incident response team can serve many functions, including investigating events, responding to events in progress, or helping secure equipment after an event has occurred. The incident response team can be mobilized to react to equipment thefts or to secure equipment after a building collapse or a fire. The incident response team can also be mobilized to respond during a natural disaster and to help secure equipment after the damage phase of a disaster passes.

There have been volumes written about how to establish a computer incident response team, but most of that has focused on cyber security issues. Many security experts have contrived very complex processes for establishing computer incident response teams, but for most organizations these teams do not necessarily have to be large and complex. The quantity of IT assets and the number of locations at which an organization has computers will largely dictate the size of the response team.

Individuals who are members of a physical IT security incident response team do not need to work full time on the team. In fact, most teams are formed out of IT staff and personnel from other divisions, and go into action when an event occurs. For most organizations this process can be reduced down to some very simple questions of who, what, where, when, and why. Key decisions to make when establishing a computer incident response team are:

- Why is the incident response team being established?
- Who is in charge of the incident response team?
- Who needs to be on team or work with the team?
- What does the team do when there is an attack?
- Where does the response team need to be to accomplish their tasks?
- When must the team respond?

Deciding who is in charge of your incident response team depends on the size of the security and IT staff your organization has in place. There should always be one person on the team who can work at the management level and be able to interact with other managers in the organization without problems. The management lead on the team in a small organization will likely be the operations director or the MIS director. In larger organizations it most likely will be a functional area manager or a security director.

In addition, a staff person from the public relations department or internal communications function could assist in communicating team needs throughout the organization. The best way to decide who needs to be on the team is to design a response process and figure out who will do what tasks during the response. Establishing procedures for what the team does when there is an incident will also help determine how many people and what types of people should be members of the team.

Among the many things that the team leaders need to establish is where the response team should be in order to accomplish their task and when the team must respond to an incident. These types of questions will vary considerably by the size, type, and geographic disbursement of computers in the organization.

The process of responding to an incident should happen very quickly. However, teams should follow documented procedures to make sure that systems are protected in accordance with many possible legal or organizational requirements. This chapter covers the basic steps response teams take when responding to a breach in physical IT security, including:

- The first report
- The confirmation process
- Mobilizing the response team

- Notifying management
- Using an alert system and informing end-users
- Preservation of evidence
- When to call law enforcement
- The return to normal operations
- Analyzing lessons learned

A model program for training IT staff, corporate security personnel, and employees who work in all departments on physical IT security procedures and incident response is provided in Chapter 8. It is important to implement such training programs because employees can become the first line of defense in protecting IT assets.

To help illustrate how the incident response process works and how entries should be made in the response team log, a case study is used in this chapter. The case involves a midsize company that was broken into over a weekend and had several computers stolen. Log entries are made for the actions of the response team on a model incident response log.

7.1   The First Report

The IT and security departments, in combination with other contributing divisions or work groups in an organization need to work together to design, launch, and support an internal reporting system. The system needs to be easy to use, and employees need to be informed about the system and trained to use the system. Above all, the system must be responsive. If employees do not feel that the IT department is responding to reports and taking them seriously, the system will quickly deteriorate and cease to function.

An internal reporting system for physical security incidents allows employees, customers, and associates to report things that they know are or suspect to be security incidents. There are several elements to a successful internal reporting system:

- Employee training to identify incidents or possible incidents
- A process for employees to send or file reports
- A process for IT or security staff to receive reports and respond

It is advisable to have multiple ways for an employee to file a report. E-mail or a web-based form are good options but they will not work if the employee's computer is not functioning. This means that a telephone contact option should also be available. The key to success in all of the contact systems is to make sure that e-mails, web-based reports, and voicemail systems are checked frequently enough to enable a rapid response.

Many organizations maintain a log of all the events that occur and the steps that the response team takes. The first things on the log of an actual event will include:

- When the first report was received
- How the first report was received
- Who performed the confirmation of the incident
- The nature of the incident
- When the incident response team was mobilized
- Who is leading the team and who is on the team

Sample physical IT security incident log entries relating to the first report phase of an incident in which computer equipment was stolen are shown in Table 7.1.

Table 7.1 *Log Entries for First Report*

Date/Time	Log Entry	Staff
August 1 6:45 A.M.	Upon entering the building CEO noticed some office doors were standing open that are normally locked after hours. She reported the unlocked doors to security and the computer help desk via voicemail.	LK
7:10 A.M.	Department manager found the same doors unlocked and discovered that several computers were missing. Manager called security and the IT department.	LK
7:16 A.M.	Security staff had just arrived in the building and went to assist in the investigation.	LK
7:30 A.M.	IT technician arrived to help determine what computers where missing.	RR

7.2 The Confirmation Process

The confirmation process is not extremely complicated. But before an entire incident response team is mobilized and IT staff, security personnel, and possibly even department managers are pulled from other tasks to initiate response, it is advisable that scope and potential magnitude of the incident be properly assessed.

The confirmation process helps to set an agenda for response. Once an incident is confirmed, the response team begins to implement procedures necessary to secure the computing environment. Once this is achieved, the incident response team follows procedures very similar to those described in the rest of this chapter. Incident log entries relating to the confirmation phase of an incident in which computer equipment was stolen are shown in Table 7.2.

Table 7.2 *Log Entries for Confirmation Process*

Date/Time	Log Entry	Staff
August1 7:45 A.M.	Positive confirmation was made of seven computers stolen from the first floor.	RR
7:47 A.M.	Two departments on the second floor called security and the IT department reporting that computers were missing.	LK
7:55 A.M.	IT technician arrived on the second floor to help determine what computers were missing.	RR
8:00 A.M.	Positive confirmation was made of five computers stolen from the second floor.	RR
8:00 A.M.	Additional report of missing equipment was received from the warehouse. (It was not computer equipment.)	TG

7.3 Mobilizing the Response Team

The practical consequences for mobilizing an incident response team will vary by organization and will depend on how the team is staffed. Generally speaking, the IT staff, security personnel, and appropriate staff from other departments are involved in a response.

If procedures similar to those that have been recommended in prior chapters of this book were developed, the departments responsible for various aspects of physical IT security have been identified. The person responsible for confirming and initiating mobilization will know whom to call based on the preestablished call list. Incident log entries relating to the mobilization phase of an incident in which computer equipment was stolen are shown in Table 7.3.

Table 7.3   *Log Entries for Mobilization*

Date/Time	Log Entry	Staff
August 1 8:05 A.M.	The computer incident response team is mobilized. Operations manager is team lead. RR will handle the IT department's response. Purchasing department is collecting information on cost of computers that were stolen. DN from CEO's office is handling internal communication. Security manager is interviewing employees.	LK
8:10 A.M.	IT help desk is determining user IDs for missing computers and is disabling all related passwords and associated user IDs for other systems, including telephones, security doors, and remote access.	RR
8:15 A.M.	IT manager went to discuss the incident with the CEO's office.	RR

7.4   **Notifying Management**

It is important that organization managers at all levels understand when an incident has occurred. Many organizations have a management notification procedure in place. Notification processes need to be customized for an organization and should take advantage of existing communications mechanisms. Notifications to management should be straightforward and nontechnical. They should also include an estimate of the magnitude of the problem. Incident log entries relating to the notification of management about an incident in which computer equipment was stolen are shown in Table 7.4.

Table 7.4 *Log Entries for Notification of Management*

Date/Time	Log Entry	Staff
August 1 8:30 A.M.	IT manager met with the CEO and her staff to discuss the incident and discuss internal communications.	LK
8:45 A.M.	Department managers were notified that all employees should take inventory of equipment to identify other equipment that may be missing.	LK
8:50 A.M.	The CEO's office staff has been assigned to work on alerting departments and employees.	LK
8:55 A.M.	The CEO wants to be updated as necessary until normal operations are restored. If she is not immediately available then we should work through her administrative assistant.	LK

7.5 Using the Alert System

An alert system has several functions. The primary function is to notify employees that an incident has occurred and what management wants employees to do to assist in the response. Another function of the alert system is to notify computer users that there may have been a compromise of computer security other than what is physically obvious.

Such alerts should provide an explanation of what is known. This type of notification process helps mobilize employees to be an effective part of the response measures.

Alerts to computer users are usually distributed through the organization's e-mail system. However, under emergency circumstances some organizations have used their public broadcast system or have distributed brightly colored flyers at the reception desk, gates, or entranceways.

The key to successfully communicating with employees at all levels is to keep things simple and easily understandable. Incident log entries relating to using an alert system about an incident in which computer equipment was stolen are shown in Table 7.5.

Table 7.5　*Log Entries Relating to Alerting Employees*

Date/Time	Log Entry	Staff
August 1 9:10 A.M.	CEO's support staff wrote a memo and sent it via e-mail and also hand distributed it throughout the company to notify users to inventory equipment to determine if other items had been stolen.	LK
9:25 A.M.	A shorter version of the memo was printed in large fonts and posted all over the building, including on all entry doors, by the vending machines, and in the restrooms.	LK
9:55 A.M.	An updated list of the computers that were stolen was confirmed and distributed to the incident response team, CEO's office, purchasing staff, and department managers.	RR

7.6　The Preservation of Evidence

It is important to preserve as much evidence as possible for use by law enforcement authorities. In the case of stolen equipment or vandalism, it is advisable that you do not disrupt the areas from where equipment was stolen or damaged. You cannot really count on a super-duper forensics team like those you see on television to descend on your building and collect evidence for three or four days. However, you should at least give the local police department the option of examining the crime scene before you start clean-up or let employees go to work in that area.

Computer incident log entries relating to the preservation of evidence in an incident that involved the theft of computer equipment are shown in Table 7.6.

Table 7.6　*Log Entries for Preservation of Evidence*

Date/Time	Log Entry	Staff
August 1 8:30 A.M.	All managers were advised to keep employees away from the desk and other spaces from which the computers and other equipment were stolen.	LK
9:10 A.M.	Memos sent out asking employees to inventory equipment also advised employees to keep out of the areas from which equipment was stolen.	LK

Table 7.6 *Log Entries for Preservation of Evidence (continued)*

Date/Time	Log Entry	Staff
10:00 A.M.	After a check of the alarm, system security staff discovered that it had been disabled over the weekend. The alarm system closet was resecured and the area around it blocked off.	LK
10:15 A.M.	The rear door of the warehouse was discovered to be unlocked and security manager suspects that is the way the stolen equipment was removed from the building. The area was blocked off until the investigation is completed.	LK
10:30 A.M.	Purchasing has determined the cost of all of the equipment that was identified as stolen.	TG

7.7   When to Call Law Enforcement

If there is an incident that should be reported to law enforcement authorities it is advisable that the senior manager in organization make the decision to report. Many organizations are hesitant to call in law enforcement because they do not know what to expect during an investigation.

Other organizations are concerned about potential scandals that could be created by an investigation or a court case. In addition, many managers feel that the expenses for legal counsel to protect the interests of the organization during a court case are excessive.

What the incident response team and organization management should expect from law enforcement and what should be done to aid in the investigation is covered in Chapter 2. Incident log entries relating to calling law enforcement because of an incident in which equipment is stolen are shown in Table 7.7.

Table 7.7 *Log Entries for Calling Law Enforcement*

Date/Time	Log Entry	Staff
August 1, 10:30 A.M.	The CEO and purchasing manager conferred with the insurance company and decided they would file a claim for replacement of the stolen equipment. The insurance company said it requires a police report be made.	TG
10:45 A.M.	The CEO called the county police department.	TG

Table 7.7   *Log Entries for Calling Law Enforcement (continued)*

Date/Time	Log Entry	Staff
11:45 A.M.	The county police department arrives and meets with the incident response team in the CEO's conference room.	TG
12:30 P.M.	The county police department examined all of the offices from where the computers and other equipment were stolen. They also examined the rear entrance of the warehouse and the alarm system closet.	TG
1:30 P.M.	The county police depart and leave a variety of forms that must be completed and brought to the police station.	TG
1:45 P.M.	The incident response team meets in the CEO's conference room to assign work to different members for completing the required police forms.	TG
4:00 P.M.	The operations director went to the police station to file the required forms.	TG

7.8   Returning to Normal Operations

The final phase of an incident response is to return to normal operations. In the case in which equipment was stolen, efforts to return to normal operations did not start until the CEO decided to file an insurance claim and the required police reports were completed. The return to normal operations phase encompasses all of those activities related to repair or replacement of equipment, restoration of files, and repairs of building damage when necessary. Incident log entries relating to returning to normal operations after an incident in which equipment was stolen are shown in Table 7.8.

Table 7.8   *Log Entries for Returning to Normal Operations*

Date/Time	Log Entry	Staff
August 2 9:30 A.M.	Replacement equipment was ordered with second day air shipping.	RR
11:00 A.M.	The rear door of the warehouse was repaired and the alarm system wiring replaced.	TG

Table 7.8 *Log Entries for Returning to Normal Operations (continued)*

Date/Time	Log Entry	Staff
1:00 P.M	Four computers were moved from an office no longer in use to the work areas of the people that had the most urgent need for computers. Software was loaded and new user accounts established for network and application access.	RR
1:45 P.M.	It was discovered that two laptops had also been stolen from a storage cabinet in on the second floor. The people that the laptops were assigned to were out of town on business and the department manager thought they had their laptops with them.	RR
2:00 P.M.	A supplemental form was filled out for the police department notifying them of the new discovery and how it was made.	TG
2:05 P.M.	The operations manager delivered the supplemental form to the police station.	TG
2:30 P.M.	The alarm system company finished repairs on the alarm system and recommended that a stronger door and lock be put on the system closet.	TG
3:00 P.M.	An insurance adjuster arrived and completed reports and the CEO signed form for the insurance claim for the stolen equipment.	TG
3:30 P.M.	The operations manager contracted with a construction company to install a new door on the alarm system closet.	TG

7.9   **Analyzing Lessons Learned**

Analyzing lessons learned is an important part of the incident response process. It is best to have such sessions as the incident is winding down so team members do not forget what they observed or experienced. It is helpful to record the comments from the team and set agenda items for various departments. It is advisable also to hold periodic reviews of the progress that has been made to accomplish those agenda items. Incident log entries relating to the analysis of lessons learned phases of an incident in which equipment was stolen are shown in Table 7.9.

Table 7.9   *Log Entries for Analyzing Lessons Learned*

Date/Time	Log Entry	Staff
August 3 1:00 P.M.	Lessons learned session was held with all members of the incident response team, the IT director, the CEO, and the CEO's assistant. Entries are listed for each participant in the session.	TG
	The security manager suggested that the use of a drive-by security patrol for after-hours be evaluated to determine if it could help prevent such an incident in the future.	TG
	The operations manager concluded that overall the response went rather well but recommended that the lapse time from when the incident was discovered until when the police were called could be reduced.	TG
	The IT department reported that there was one problem they had deleting user accounts because the paperwork on a new employee was misfiled and the department has decided to implement a new procedure to better deal with the records for new employees.	TG
	The purchasing director who collected the information on the cost of all the equipment reported that there was a problem finding cost on equipment that was purchased more than three years ago, before the new inventory system was implemented. The purchasing department is evaluating how to get some older but more valuable equipment into the computer-based inventory system.	TG
	The department managers from which the equipment was stolen expressed concern about how long it took to get computers replaced for the employees who most urgently needed them.	TG
	The IT department reported that one of the reasons it took so long to get urgent needs met was not simply because of a lack of computer equipment, but also because many files on the computers of the users with the most urgent need were not backed up on a routine basis, making the process take longer than expected. The IT department is evaluating new back-up procedures for desktop computers.	TG

Table 7.9   *Log Entries for Analyzing Lessons Learned (continued)*

Date/Time	Log Entry	Staff
	The CEO expressed overall satisfaction with the incident response but asked that the team have a follow-up meeting in three weeks to discuss the status of the items that required attention.	TG
	A date for the follow-up meeting was set and the meeting was adjourned.	TG

7.10   The Role of the Incident Response Team During Disasters

The physical IT security incident response team can have a significant role in responding to a natural disaster or a deliberate damaging incident. The response team also can play a role in evaluating and executing mitigation efforts. This involvement will make the team members more aware of the environment in which they may need to respond to an incident.

There are several high-level activities that occur during an emergency response. The physical IT security incident response team will be primarily responsible for property protection. Emergency response activities include:

- Direction and control, which is a system for managing resources, analyzing information, and making decisions in an emergency

- Communications that are needed to report emergencies, to warn personnel of the danger, to keep families and off-duty employees informed about what's happening at the facility, to coordinate response actions, and to keep in contact with customers and suppliers

- Life safety, which is protecting the health and safety of everyone in the facility

- Property protection, which is protecting facilities, equipment, and vital records, and is essential to restoring operations once an emergency has occurred

- Community outreach, which is maintaining the facility's relationship with the community and will influence your ability to protect personnel and property and return to normal operations

- Recovery of operations and restoration of business facilities

- Administration and logistics, which is the maintenance of complete and accurate records at all times to ensure a more efficient emergency response and recovery

The Federal Emergency Management Agency (FEMA), which is part of the Department of Homeland Security's Emergency Preparedness and Response Directorate, has recommended many steps that organizations can take to be prepared for catastrophic events. Several of these recommendations focus on or affect the physical security of IT assets. Those recommendations are summarized in the following paragraphs.

There are several types of hazards for which the response team should be specifically prepared, including:

- Fire

- Hazardous materials incidents

- Floods and flash floods

- Severe weather, including hurricanes, tornadoes, and winter storms

- Earthquakes

FEMA considers fire to be the most common of all the hazards. To better protect IT assets from fire damage the physical IT security incident response team should assist in the following fire prevention and response efforts:

- Inspect your facility for fire hazards that could damage IT assets

- Act as fire wardens to monitor equipment and facility shutdown processes and coordinate evacuation procedures

- Evaluate preventive maintenance schedules that can help keep equipment operating safely

- Evaluate placement of fire extinguishers and train employees to properly use fire extinguishers to protect equipment and facilities
- Identify and mark all shutoffs so that electrical power, gas, or water can be shut off quickly by fire wardens or responding personnel and thus limit damage to equipment

The physical IT security incident response team also should be prepared for hazardous materials incidents. A hazardous material spill or release can pose a risk to life, health, or property. Hazardous materials are substances that are either flammable or combustible, explosive, toxic, noxious, corrosive, oxidizable, irritants, or radioactive. There are a number of federal laws that regulate hazardous materials, including:

- The Superfund Amendments and Reauthorization Act of 1986 (SARA)
- The Resource Conservation and Recovery Act of 1976 (RCRA)
- The Hazardous Materials Transportation Act (HMTA)
- The Occupational Safety and Health Act (OSHA)
- The Toxic Substances Control Act (TSCA) and the Clean Air Act

Title III of SARA regulates the packaging, labeling, handling, storage, and transportation of hazardous materials. The law requires facilities to furnish information about the quantities and health effects of materials used at the facility, and to promptly notify local and state officials whenever a significant release of hazardous materials occurs.

In addition to on-site hazards, the physical IT security incident response team should be aware of the potential for an offsite incident affecting your operations. This includes being aware of hazardous materials used in facility processes and in the construction of the physical plant. Detailed definitions as well as lists of hazardous materials can be obtained from the Environmental Protection Agency (EPA) and the Occupational Safety and Health Administration (OSHA).

Only trained specialists should handle hazardous materials incidents. However, the physical IT security incident response team can assist in the following ways when your organization is developing a hazardous materials plan:

- Obtaining material safety data sheets (MSDS) for all hazardous materials at your location

- Identifying and labeling all hazardous materials stored, handled, produced, and disposed of by your facility that could damage equipment

- Working with the local fire department in developing appropriate response procedure

- Training employees to recognize and report hazardous material spills and releases

- Organizing and training the incident response team to confine and control hazardous material spills in accordance with applicable regulations

- Identifying highways, railroads, and waterways near your facility used for the transportation of hazardous materials and determining how a transportation accident near your facility could affect your operations or damage equipment

FEMA contends that floods are the most common and widespread natural disasters. Most communities in the United States can experience some degree of flooding after spring rains, heavy thunderstorms, or winter snow thaws. Most floods develop slowly over a period of days. However, flash floods can develop in a matter of minutes when there are intense storms or dam failures.

To better protect IT assets from flood damage the physical IT security incident response team can assist in the following ways when your organization is developing a flood safety plan or responding to a flood:

- Documenting the history of flooding in your area and the elevation of your facility in relation to streams, rivers, and dams

- Reviewing community emergency plans, learning the evacuation routes, and locating higher ground in case of a flood

- Developing and executing plans for the emergency evacuation of equipment

- Inspecting areas in your facility subject to flooding, identifying equipment that can be moved to a higher location, and moving equipment when necessary

- Having check valves installed to prevent water from entering where utility and sewer lines enter the facility

- Supporting efforts to reinforce walls to resist water pressure or sealing walls to prevent or reduce seepage

- Supporting the construction of watertight walls around equipment or work areas within the facility that are particularly susceptible to flood damage

- Supporting the construction of floodwalls or levees outside the facility to keep floodwaters away

- Supporting the installation of permanent watertight doors, movable floodwalls, and permanent pumps to remove flood waters

There are several types of severe weather that can severely damage buildings or equipment, disrupt operations, or endanger the lives of employees. These include hurricanes, tornadoes, and winter storms.

Hurricanes are severe tropical storms with sustained winds of 74 miles per hour or greater and can reach 160 miles per hour and extend inland for hundreds of miles. Hurricanes bring torrential rains, storm surges of ocean water that crashes into land as the storm approaches, and can spawn tornadoes. The hurricane season lasts from June through November.

Tornadoes are incredibly violent local storms that extend to the ground with whirling winds that can reach 300 mph. Mostly spawned from powerful thunderstorms, tornadoes can uproot trees and buildings and turn harmless objects into deadly missiles in a matter of seconds. Damage paths can be in excess of one mile wide and 50 miles long. Tornadoes can occur in any state, but occur more frequently in the Midwest, Southeast, and Southwest. They occur with little or no warning.

Severe winter storms bring heavy snow, ice, strong winds, and freezing rain. Winter storms can prevent employees and customers from reaching the facility, leading to a temporary shutdown until roads are cleared. Heavy snow and ice can also cause structural damage and power outages.

To better protect IT assets from damage during severe weather the physical IT security incident response team can assist in the following ways when your organization is developing a severe weather safety plan or responding to severe weather:

- Developing and executing equipment and facility shutdown procedures

- Developing and executing plans to move computers and other items within your facility or to another location

- Surveying your facility and devising plans to protect equipment and structures

- Supporting plans to protect windows with storm shutters

- Evaluating the need for remote backup systems

- Supporting the acquisition of portable pumps to remove floodwater

- Supporting the installation of alternate power sources such as generators or gasoline-powered pumps and battery-powered emergency lighting

Earthquakes occur most frequently west of the Rocky Mountains, although historically the most violent earthquakes have occurred in the central United States. Earthquakes can seriously damage buildings and their contents; disrupt gas, electric, and telephone services; and trigger landslides, avalanches, flash floods, fires, and huge ocean waves called tsunamis. Aftershocks can occur for weeks following an earthquake.

In many buildings, the greatest danger to people in an earthquake is when equipment and nonstructural elements such as ceilings, partitions, windows, and lighting fixtures shake loose.

To better protect IT assets from damage during earthquakes the physical IT security incident response team can assist in the following ways when your organization is developing an earthquake safety plan or restoring operations after an earthquake:

- Having your facility inspected by a structural engineer to identify vulnerabilities

- Developing and prioritizing strengthening measures, including steel bracing to frames, sheer walls to frames, strengthening columns and building foundations, or replacing unreinforced brick filler walls

- Supporting adherence with safety codes when constructing a facility or making major renovations

- Assessing the potential for damage to nonstructural systems such as air conditioning, communications, and manufacturing control systems that can be caused by earthquakes

- Inspecting your facility for any item that could fall, spill, break, or move during an earthquake, and taking steps to reduce these hazards

- Determining how to secure shelves, filing cabinets, tall furniture, desktop equipment, computers, printers, copiers and light fixtures

- Determining how to secure fixed equipment and heavy machinery to the floor or placing larger equipment on casters and attached to tethers that attach to the wall

- Supporting the installation of safety glass where appropriate

- Determining how to secure large utility and process piping

- Keeping copies of design drawings of the facility to be used in assessing the facility's safety after an earthquake

7.11 Action Steps to Improve Physical IT Security

The material in this chapter shows the basic steps in responding to a physical IT security incident. As steps are taken to improve physical security of IT assets, managers, planners, and technical staff should understand the following principles:

- Physical IT security incidents should be responded to as quickly as possible.

- The response team should follow procedures and thoroughly document the incident and how they responded.

- Rapid incident response requires the cooperation of several departments and should be supported by all managers.

- Having a complete inventory of all computers and networking equipment in the organization and ready access to cost information can help support quick action when law enforcement is called or insurance claims are filed.

- It is advisable to hold a lessons learned session after each incident to quickly incorporate those lessons into new or modified procedures and set an agenda for other changes that may help deter or prevent a similar incident in the future.

- A physical IT security incident response team can play a role in planning for and responding to a disaster.

There are several steps that organizations can take to help improve the physical security of IT assets. Recommended steps are included at the end of each chapter. The action steps listed in Table 7.10 are designed to help an organization develop or improve incident response procedures.

Table 7.10   *Action Steps to Improve Physical IT Security*

Step Number	Action Step
7.01	Assign a subgroup of the physical IT security working group to evaluate existing incident response procedures in your organization to determine if they meet the needs of responding to a physical IT security incident.
7.02	Assign a subgroup of the physical IT security working group to recommend amendments to your existing incident response procedures or develop new procedures for response.
7.03	Select the members of your incident response team from those departments that have various responsibilities for physical IT security (as was recommended in Chapter 4).
7.04	Have the members of the incident response team designate an alternate from their department to serve as a team member in their absence.
7.05	Convene the members of the incident response team and their alternates to review the response procedures.
7.06	Review the first report, confirmation, and mobilization procedures to determine if they are adequate in scope to mobilize a response to an incident.
7.07	Review the process to notify management, alert departments, and inform end-users to determine if they are adequate in scope to support a response to an incident.
7.08	Review the procedures for preserving evidence of a crime to determine if they are adequate in scope to meet the needs of reporting a crime to law enforcement agencies.
7.09	Review the procedures for notifying law enforcement that a computer crime has occurred to determine if they are adequate in scope to meet the needs of the organization.
7.10	Review the processes of analyzing and acting on lessons learned from an incident to determine if they can help the organization improve response.
7.11	Hold a tabletop simulation of an incident and have the members of the response team describe what they would do to respond. Walk through the incident step by step as described in this chapter.

Table 7.10 *Action Steps to Improve Physical IT Security (continued)*

Step Number	Action Step
7.12	Review the results of the tabletop simulation of an incident and have the members recommend changes to the incident response plan if necessary.
7.13	Evaluate the role the incident response team should play in planning for or responding to a natural disaster or a deliberate damaging incident and develop appropriate procedures.

Model Training Program for Organization Staff

Education, training, and awareness are all necessary for the successful implementation of any information security program, according to the Critical Infrastructure Assurance Office of the United States Government. Although these three elements are related, they involve distinctly different levels of learning.

Awareness is not training but is a prerequisite to it. Its purpose is to focus attention on security. Awareness programs are generally well established within organizations. An example of an awareness campaign would be the plethora of posters visible in most federal buildings, reminding users that passwords are not to be shared.

Awareness provides a baseline of security knowledge for all users, regardless of job duties or position. The level of security awareness required of a summer intern program assistant is the same as that needed by the CEO, CIO, or a division manager in organization. IT security awareness programs should be tied directly to security policy development and the organization's computer security incident response capability.

Training is geared to understanding the security aspects of the particular IT systems and applications for which the trainee is responsible. Security training should take into account the uniqueness of each system and application.

Education differs from training in both breadth and depth of knowledge and skills acquired. Security education, including formal courses and certification programs, is most appropriate for an organization's designated security specialists. This chapter discusses how you can achieve your training needs, including:

- Training for IT and security professionals
- The basics of training

- Building awareness about physical security for IT assets
- Training employees on how to identify potential threats
- What employees should do if they see suspicious behavior
- What employees should expect from different departments
- How your internal alert system works
- Administrative management of training programs

8.1   Training for IT and Security Professionals

Training for IT and security professionals is essential to effectively implement a physical IT security program. How IT and security departments are staffed will dictate many of the training needs. In addition to basic security skills, the IT and security staff responsible for physical IT security need knowledge in the following areas.

- Understanding the value of computer security and physical security measures
- Knowledge of basic security management practices
- How to install, configure, and deploy physical security products selected by the organization
- How to create and implement policies and procedures
- How to audit, test, and monitor compliance with physical security policies and procedures
- How to respond to a physical IT security incident
- How to work with other IT and security staff to improve computer security
- How to train end-users on physical IT security measures
- How to communicate with managers and end-users during an incident response
- How to preserve evidence for law enforcement of personnel actions
- How to work with law enforcement on computer security incident investigations
- Ways to monitor emerging threats and evaluate vulnerabilities

There are many sources of training that can be helpful to improve computer security in general. Many junior colleges and community colleges are now offering short courses or term-long courses on computer security and physical security. The short courses are often one or two days in length and are relatively inexpensive. The semester-long courses certainly do require more commitment on the part of the person being trained but they may also provide more in-depth learning experiences.

Selecting which type of training is needed and the best source of training that will be helpful to an organization will depend on several factors, including how many staff are in the IT and security departments and how specialized those individuals are in their daily jobs. Many organizations have decided to have certified security personnel who have undergone extensive training and who have passed an examination to demonstrate their skill level. Smaller to midsize organizations probably do not require nor can afford certified security staff. Large organizations tend to choose certified people because they can be assured of a minimum competency level.

8.2 The Basics of Training

Developing training programs does not need to be complicated. The key thing to remember is that the tone and the style of the training program should be good for the organization. The individuals who lead the training session need to be personable and able to communicate with people from a wide variety of backgrounds and education levels. They also need to be able to talk to people who may be clerks, middle managers, professional specialists, or upper-level managers.

It is not likely that the smartest IT person in your organization will make the best trainer for this subject. However, it does help to have a staff person who works in computer security and has responsibility for physical measures to help with the training sessions. Several of the modules in this model program need IT department support during the development process. In addition, IT staff can present part of the material or they can help with questions and answers.

One of the best ways to deliver a training session is to have that ideal person who can communicate with all sorts of people explain the basic nontechnical material. Then have an IT specialist to explain the material that requires a more technical presentation and requires greater knowledge to answer questions about the material.

Both trainers and trainees have preferred styles and it is difficult to accommodate all people when designing a training session. There are several things that can help training go smoothly and be more enjoyable:

- Take a participatory approach and facilitate interaction during the training sessions.

- Have colorful and entertaining visual aids.

- Serve refreshments.

- Hold sessions in a pleasant environment.

- Hold sessions in well-ventilated areas.

- Provide comfortable seating.

- Have all the materials, handouts, and any forms that employees must sign well organized and easy to distribute during the session.

- Have ink pens available for employees to sign forms. (Let them keep the pens if they want; they cost less than a dollar each.)

- Provide sufficient stretch breaks.

8.3   Building Awareness About Physical Security for IT Assets

The first step for any type of training is to explain why it is important that employees learn what is being taught. Employees will have a greater appreciation of what they are learning and of the things you want them to do if they can be sold on the importance of the new knowledge and skills. This should be a relatively long module in the training program. This module also should be able to stand alone and be used as an awareness building seminar.

It is the responsibility of the training designers and the trainers to develop and deliver the message of importance. This responsibility can be viewed as an evangelistic recruiting mission. There are several good selling points for physical IT security training.

- There are legal and regulatory requirements with which organizations such as banking companies and defense contractors must comply. (Specific regulations and laws can be quoted in the training material.)

- The mission statement of the organization can be used as a focal point if it emphasizes service to customers that should be high quality and continuously available. (The mission statement of the organization can be used in the training material.)

- The potential consequences of physical damage to IT assets are very serious and can be described in the training, including:

  1. Immediate economic impact can include damage to systems that requires human intervention to repair or replace, disruption of business operations, and delays in transactions and cash flow.

  2. Short-term economic impact can include loss of contracts with other organizations in supply chains or the loss of retail sales, negative impact on an organization's reputation, and a hindrance to developing new business.

  3. Long-term economic impact can include a decline in market valuation, erosion of investor confidence, decline in stock price, and reduced goodwill value.

- Explain the nature of the threat by using material from Chapter 1 to illustrate the type of people who damage IT assets, including: disgruntled employees and angry former employees; activists who oppose your organization; vandals who damage for fun; saboteurs who work for profit; thieves and spies; domestic and international terrorists.

- Use interesting facts and figures to illustrate the magnitude of the problem. Examples include:

  1. The theft of computers has been increasing for several years and costs organizations over one billion dollars per year.

  2. The FBI reports that 97% of stolen computer equipment is never recovered.

  3. More than 500,000 laptops are stolen every year.

There are several visual aids that can be used during this part of the training session (see Table 8.1). Any or all of the types of impacts can be included as bulleted items in training material for your organization. The methods of measurement are widely recognized and used by organizations all over the world.

Another interesting and attention getting visual aide is a table that illustrates the potential cost of an outage because centralized servers and network or communications equipment has been physically damaged to the point that it requires repair or replacement.

Table 8.1   *Impact of Physical Damage to IT Assets*

Direct damage to your computer systems
Cost to repair damage or restore your systems and functionality
Decrease in productivity of your employees
Delays in your order processing or customer service
Decrease in productivity in your customer's organization because of delays in your organization
Delays in customer's business because of delays in your organization
Negative impact on local economies where disrupted organizations are located
Negative impact on value for individual investors in disrupted organization
Negative impact on value of investment funds holding disrupted organization securities
Negative impact on regional economies where disrupted organizations, customers, or investors are located
Negative impact on national economies where disrupted organizations, customers, or investors are located

Source: *Implementing Homeland Security in Enterprise IT*, Michael Erbschloe
(Boston: Digital Press, 2003)

This was discussed in Chapter 1 by using examples that show an average cost of an employee hour that includes salaries, benefits, facilities, and overhead costs. The examples also showed how the potential economic impact of lost productivity is calculated along with the total cost of a one-day outage and a three-day outage.

Table 8.2 is a sample visual aide that shows the potential impact on your organization if employees do not have access to computers and communications equipment to do their work for one day (8 working hours).

Table 8.3 is a sample visual aide that shows the potential impact on your organization if employees do not have access to computers and communications equipment to do their work for three days (24 working hours).

Table 8.2 *Cost of a One-Day Outage*

Variable	Description	Quantity
A	Number of employees who do work that requires access to computers & communications equipment	Enter your employee count here
B	Average cost of employee hour including salaries, benefits, facilities, and overhead	Enter your employee cost here
C	Potential lost productivity for one day of system outages (A * B * 8)	Enter your loss here
D	Cost to restore or replace damaged equipment	???
	Total cost of outage	C + D

Table 8.3 *Cost of a Three-Day Outage*

Variable	Description	Quantity
A	Number of employees who do work that requires access to computers & communications equipment	Enter your employee count here
B	Average cost of employee hour, including salaries, benefits, facilities, and overhead	Enter your employee cost here
C	Potential lost productivity for one day of system outages (A * B * 24)	Enter your loss here
D	Cost to restore or replace damaged equipment	???
	Total cost of outage	C + D

8.3.1 Testing and Evaluating the Module

Once the training material for this module has been assembled and put into the format of Power Point slides or handouts, the presentation should be rehearsed and tested. This can be done with employees or friends and associates of the training developers and trainers. The key thing to test this module for is its selling power. The evaluators should be asked to answer the following questions:

1. Does the material convince you that learning about physical IT security is important?

2. Does the material convince you that our organization takes physical IT security seriously?

3. Does the material motivate you to participate in the training?

4. Does the material inspire you to help the organization protect IT assets?

5. Did you understand all of the material? (If no, then seek clarification on what was not understandable.)

6. What part of the presentation did you like the most?

7. Which slide or graphic did you like the most?

8. What part of the presentation did you like the least?

9. Which slide or graphic did you like the least?

10. Should anything be added to the presentation?

11. Should anything be taken out of the presentation?

8.4 How to Identify Potential Threats and Vulnerabilities

Training employees to identify threats and vulnerabilities involves building a basic understanding of who or what can pose a threat, what the procedures or methods are to protect IT assets from those threats, and what may contribute to or cause a new vulnerability. This should be a relatively long module in the training program.

The first topic to cover in this module is threats and countermeasures. The second topic is basic security procedures and conditions that employees should be aware of and for which violations should be reported. Power Point slides or handouts can be developed to cover each type of threat and what your organization does to help mitigate that threat.

Recommended slides and sample content are presented in this section. You should select only content that is relevant to your physical IT security goals. Sample slides are provided for all of the threat areas covered in Chapter 1 and most of the types of IT assets for which security procedures are recommended. Bear in mind that the samples are generic and you should custom tailor all of the content to your organization, threat analysis, and security procedures.

8.4.1 Slides for Disgruntled and Angry Former Employees

Slide One

Disgruntled employees or angry former employees can cause considerable physical damage to equipment. This is often referred to as the insider threat, or former insider threat. In situations in which employees plan to do damage to the facilities or equipment of an organization they have the advantages of:

- Knowledge of facility layout and design
- Familiarity with the location of sensitive or expensive equipment
- Duplicate keys that allow them easy access to buildings
- Knowledge of access codes for alarm systems
- The ability to gain access to buildings with the aid of a friend or relative who is still employed by an organization
- Knowledge of organization habits such as shift changes or which doors are not secured during working hours

Slide Two

Explain the procedures you have in place to help prevent damage from insiders or former insiders. Examples could include:

- Security is notified when an employee has been terminated or suspended.
- Access to facilities by nonemployees is limited.
- Get keys back from terminated or suspended employees.
- Change the locks for which any angry former employee had keys.
- Change key codes to electronic doors immediately after an employee has been terminated or suspended.
- Disable user rights for computers or communications systems held by former or suspended employees.

8.4.2   Slides for Social and Political Activists

Slide One

Political or social activists have caused damage to many organizations. This is often referred to as the outsider threat. Activists who plan to do damage to the facilities or equipment have the following advantages:

- They are often highly motivated and intelligent people.
- They usually plan and organize their attacks.
- They get support from national or international groups.
- They have skills to break and enter buildings.
- They collect considerable amounts of data about an organization to identify specific locations to attack.
- They are not very concerned about being arrested or prosecuted, which makes laws ineffective as a deterrent.

Slide Two

Explain the procedures you have in place to help prevent damage from outsiders. Examples could include:

- Security is notified of activist group threats.
- Primary services for the building are secured.
- Critical or sensitive information is secured within the building.
- Circulation of information about activities is minimized.
- The profile of the facility is minimized by limiting identification in scientific papers, press releases, or public mention by researchers or executives about the facility.
- Security works with law enforcement agencies.

8.4.3   Slides for Random Vandals

Slide One

There is a threat of damage by random vandals who do not hold any specific animosities toward an organization. Vandals demonstrate several common behaviors, including:

- Vandals are not deterred by laws against physical destruction or vandalism.

- Vandals are often driven by peer pressure to perform antisocial actions.

- Vandals have little consideration for the effects of their actions.

- Vandals often attack in small groups using one or more members as scouts to test security or be lookouts.

- Vandals usually perform random acts of destruction and will damage those things that are the easiest targets.

Slide Two

Explain the procedures you have in place to help prevent damage from vandals. Examples could include:

- Security staff are kept informed of recent or ongoing vandal activity in areas around our facility.

- Basic building security functions such as night lighting, closed circuit cameras to monitor activities, and intrusion detection systems that activate alarms are in use.

- Signs warning of no trespassing and rewards for information leading to the arrest of individuals that damage property are posted.

- Security works with local law enforcement agencies to support community watch programs and other crime reduction efforts.

8.4.4   Slides for Professional Saboteurs

Slide One

Saboteurs usually hold specific animosities toward an organization or an organization that has facilities adjacent to or near your facilities. Many saboteurs work for financial gain, or in the time of war work for a combination of financial gain and political allegiance. Other saboteurs may be part of a larger extortion scheme. Saboteurs share many characteristics, including:

- Saboteurs for hire are often well-trained individuals who employ arson or explosive techniques to cause damage.

- Saboteurs often conduct extensive research about organizations and their facilities before they strike.

- Saboteurs are usually skilled at eluding security forces and local law enforcement.

Slide Two

Explain the procedures you have in place to help prevent damage from saboteurs. Examples could include:

- Security staff are kept aware of any known saboteurs who may be targeting the organization.

- If specific threats or extortion schemes are detected, the FBI or other appropriate law enforcement agency will be notified.

- The internal layout of a building or facility is not clearly labeled.

- Key code or other locks secure areas such as server rooms, telecommunications closets, or data processing centers.

- Surveillance cameras are used in areas such as server rooms, telecommunications closets, and data processing centers.

8.4.5   Slides for Thieves and Spies

Slide One

Thieves and industrial spies usually do not want to cause damage but prefer to gain access to systems to retrieve and steal data and information. Some thieves or spies may also be part of a larger extortion scheme. When thieves or spies plan to steal data or information:

- Like saboteurs, they often work for hire and are well-trained individuals who are willing to go to great lengths to obtain the data or information they are seeking.

- They often conduct extensive research about organizations and their facilities.

- They are usually skilled at eluding security forces and local law enforcement.

- They have supporters who provide them with financial resources to enable long-term operations.

Slide Two

Explain the procedures you have in place to help prevent damage from thieves and spies. Examples could include:

- Security tracks known thieves or spies who may be a threat.
- Security works with the FBI or other appropriate law enforcement organizations.
- Key people are trained to resist social engineering methods to infiltrate or obtain information.
- Paper is shredded or burned and electronic media are destroyed before disposal.

8.4.6   Slides for Domestic and International Terrorists

Slide One

Domestic terrorists include hate groups, extreme militants, or groups opposed to the existence of the nation or society as it is currently organized and structured. International terrorists are a different type of threat from domestic terrorists because of their willingness to die during an attack. Terrorists are a considerably different type of threat from the other types of attackers because:

- Terrorists tend to study vulnerabilities that they can exploit when they plan an attack.
- Terrorists often use extreme measures and have little regard for human life during their attack.
- Terrorists are not deterred by laws nor are they compliant with the social norms of the society against which they wish to retaliate.
- Many terrorists tend to be driven by a hatred for those they are attacking.
- Many terrorists are willing to die during an attack.
- Many international terrorists are also rewarded indirectly when their families receive cash or privilege.

Slide Two

Explain the procedures you have in place to help prevent damage from terrorists. Examples could include:

- Security staff seeks information on any potential terrorist attacks.

- Security works with local law enforcement agencies to determine if terrorists are a threat to our organization or organizations with nearby facilities.

- Technology that is an attractive target for terrorists is not located in buildings with occupants.

- Technology is not located in buildings that are near attractive targets such as government buildings, iconic properties, major commercial centers, or major transportation centers.

- We conducted a vulnerability assessment of our buildings to terrorist attacks and implemented countermeasures.

- We developed and enforce procedures to control internal building parking, underground parking garages, and access to service areas and loading docks.

8.4.7   Slides for Natural Disasters

Slide One

There are two primary types of protection that must be accomplished in the event of natural disasters. The first is to ensure that the natural disaster in and of itself does not damage IT equipment. The second is to ensure that the equipment is securable if evacuation of a facility or community is required because of the severity of the disaster.
Insert analysis of frequency of natural disasters at your location.

Slide Two

Explain the procedures you have in place to help prevent damage from natural disaster. Examples could include:

- IT equipment is located in a place that is the least susceptible to flooding.

- The facility is reinforced against leakage.

- There is a removal plan for IT assets in the event that a building is damaged to the point at which it cannot be utilized.

- Procedures are in place to shut down equipment and secure facilities in the event that personnel must be evacuated.

- There is an offsite backup location for duplicate media, documentation, and data.

8.4.8 Slides for Data Center Security

Slide One

The data center is our primary IT asset and we follow several basic procedures to keep it secure, including:

- Access is controlled and visitors and service personnel must sign in and be escorted.

- Utility systems, including air-conditioning, power supplies, network connections, and emergency power systems, are secured.

- Logs are kept of all equipment that include serial numbers and configuration information.

- Environmental settings are controlled for equipment rooms.

- All incoming and outgoing equipment, documents, and supplies are signed in and out.

- All incoming packages are inspected and opened before they are brought into the data center.

- Printed materials and used magnetic media are disposed of in accordance with specific procedures.

8.4.9 Slides for Wiring and Cabling

Slide One

Wiring and cabling is protected to prevent unauthorized access through the implementation of several procedures:

- Access to wiring and cabling areas is controlled and monitored.

- Steel doors and locks secure wiring and cabling areas.

- Service providers are monitored when and if they need to access wiring and cabling areas.

- Maintenance and access logs are kept for wiring and cabling areas.

8.4.10 Slides for Remote and Mobile Computing

Slide One

We have several physical security procedures for remote computing devices, including mobile computing devices.

- Users are automatically logged off the host system when it is not being used.

- User profiles and passwords are strictly managed on remote computing devices.

- We recommend physical access controls for remote and mobile computing devices.

- We use property tags and identification systems for mobile computing devices.

- Remote and mobile users must go through training before they can be authorized to access our systems.

8.4.11 Slides for Desktop Computers

Slide One

Desktop computers pose several types of security problems, and we have developed procedures to keep unauthorized persons from removing, moving, opening, or tampering with desktop computers, including:

- Placement and protection of equipment within offices or other work areas

- Protection for cabling, plugs, and other wires that connect the devices to network

- Users are automatically logged off the host system when they are not being used

- Environmental and structural protection
- Property tags and other identification systems
- Security for computer cases to deter unauthorized entry into systems or removal or installation of items such as memory, boards, ports, etc.
- Protection from electrical surges or power outages
- Proper disposal of and used equipment

8.4.12 Slides for Department-Based Servers

Slide One

Servers located in department offices are protected by several procedures to keep unauthorized persons from removing, moving, opening, or tampering with components, including:

- How server areas are protected in offices or other work areas
- Protection for cabling, plugs, and other wires that connect the devices to networks or to local devices
- Property tags and other identification systems
- Security for department-based server cases to deter unauthorized entry into systems or removal or installation of items such as memory, boards, ports, etc.
- Theft deterrent procedures including lockdown and enclosure security
- Protection from electrical surges or power outages
- Proper disposal of used equipment

8.4.13 Slides for Telecom and Datacom Equipment

Slide One

Telecom and datacom equipment includes switches, routers, hubs, telephones, PBXs, voicemail systems, and printer sharing equipment. Regardless of where it is located, it is covered by one of several security procedures, including:

- Placement and protection of equipment within offices, other work areas, wiring and cabling areas, and in the data center

- Property tags and other identification systems
- Steel doors and locks used to equipment areas
- Alarms or monitoring systems
- Controlled access to telecom and datacom equipment areas
- Monitoring service providers when they need to access equipment areas

8.4.14 Testing and Evaluating the Module

Once the training material for this module has been assembled and put into the format of Power Point slides or handouts, the presentation should be rehearsed and tested. This can be done with employees or friends and associates of the training developers and trainers. The key thing to test this module for is if it expands the understanding of threats, procedures, and vulnerabilities. The evaluators should be asked to answer the following questions:

1. Does the material explain what the threats are to your organization?

2. Does the material adequately cover procedures that employees should know about?

3. Does the material increase the understanding of vulnerabilities?

4. Does the material inspire you to help the organization protect IT assets?

5. Did you understand all of the material? (If no, then seek clarification on what was not understandable.)

6. What part of the presentation did you like the most?

7. Which slide or graphic did you like the most?

8. What part of the presentation did you like the least?

9. Which slide or graphic did you like the least?

10. Should anything be added to the presentation?

11. Should anything be taken out of the presentation?

8.5 Reporting Suspicious Behavior or Security Violations

It is also advisable to train employees to routinely observe whether or not physical IT security procedures are being followed. Once IT and security staff understand what the procedures are, they can observe compliance with those procedures on a daily basis. They should report problems that they observe.

This module should be relatively short and should cover your suspicious behavior and security violation reports. Topics to cover include the following:

- Explain security violation reporting procedures.

- What should employees do if they see suspicious behavior?

- How and to whom should employees report suspicious behavior?

- If you use a form like the one in Figure 8.1, you should distribute copies of the form in this part of the training and explain how to complete the form and where the form should be sent.

- How are suspicious behavior and security violation reports handled by security?

Figure 8.1
Sample Procedure Violation Report

Date	Reporting Employee
Procedure name	Procedure number
Who violated the procedure (if known)	
Reason for the violation (if known)	
Details of the violation	
Training status of the violator (if known)	Date of last revision of the procedure

8.5.1   Testing and Evaluating the Module

Once the training material for this module has been assembled and put into the format of Power Point slides or handouts, the presentation should be rehearsed and tested. The test audience for this module should include both employees who are familiar with the suspicious behavior and security violation reporting process and also people who are not familiar with the process. This mix of test audiences allows training developers to test the accuracy and clarity of the material and if the presentation is understandable by those who are not familiar with the process.

The key thing to test this module for is how well it explains how the suspicious behavior and security violation report process works. The evaluators should be asked to answer the following questions:

1. How well does the presentation explain each step in the suspicious behavior and security violation reports process?

2. Did you understand all of the material? (If no, then seek clarification on what was not understandable.)

3. Does the material inspire you to help the organization deal with suspicious behavior and security violations?

4. Was the material too technical?

5. What part of the presentation did you like the most?

6. Which slide or graphic did you like the most?

7. What part of the presentation did you like the least?

8. Which slide or graphic did you like the least?

9. Should anything be added to the presentation?

10. Should anything be taken out of the presentation?

8.6   What to Expect from Different Departments

Employees will feel more involved in the efforts to improve and maintain physical IT security if they are made aware of what happens when there is an incident and how the response process works. This module does not have to go into great detail but should explain the process from beginning to end. The module should be relatively short.

An individual from the IT department and someone from the security department who works on the incident response team should help develop the content for this module. The material should reflect the operating procedures of your organization.

Slides should be made to explain the steps in the response process as it was covered in Chapter 7. This module should be customized to explain the incident response process you have developed in your organization but should include topics similar to the following:

- The first report

- The confirmation process

- Mobilizing the response team

- Notifying management

- Using an alert system and informing end-users

- The preservation of evidence

- When to call law enforcement

- The return to normal operations

- Analyzing lessons learned

Each of these areas can be covered with one or two Power Point slides. If a staff person from the IT or security department is presenting this module, the printed material can be complemented with anecdotal information. People do tend to like to tell and hear war stories.

The key thing to bear in mind about this module is that employees being trained on what is expected of them and how they can help during incident response need to have the information presented in a very straightforward and easy to understand manner. Because the information in this module is organization specific, it is important to make sure that the information reflects the reality of what happens during a computer incident response.

8.6.1   Testing and Evaluating the Module

Once the training material for this module has been assembled and put into the format of Power Point slides or handouts, the presentation should be rehearsed and tested. The test audience for this module should include both employees who are familiar with the computer incident response process and people who are not familiar with the process. This mix of test audiences allows training developers to test the accuracy and clarity of the material and whether or not the presentation is understandable by those who are not familiar with the process.

The key thing to test this module for is how well it explains how the computer incident response process works. The evaluators should be asked to answer the following questions:

1. How well does the presentation explain each step in the incident response process?

2. Did you understand all of the material? (If no, then seek clarification on what was not understandable.)

3. Does the material inspire you to help the organization monitor physical security?

4. Was the material too technical?

5. What part of the presentation did you like the most?

6. Which slide or graphic did you like the most?

7. What part of the presentation did you like the least?

8. Which slide or graphic did you like the least?

9. Should anything be added to the presentation?

10. Should anything be taken out of the presentation?

8.7   How the Internal Alert System Works

An alert system has several functions. The primary function is to notify employees that an incident has occurred and what management wants employees to do to assist in the response. Another function of the alert system is to notify computer users that there may have been a compromise of computer security other than what is physically obvious.

The purpose of this module is to explain to employees how the internal alert system works in your organization. This module should be very short and cover topics similar to the following:

- Under what conditions employees may receive alerts

- What employees should do when they receive an alert

- How alerts will be sent (e-mail, memos, flyers, etc.)

- What if anything is likely to change in day-to-day operation when an alert is sent

- Who is authorized to send out an alert
- The process of ending an alert
- The confidentiality of alerts, if applicable

8.7.1 Testing and Evaluating the Module

Once the training material for this module has been assembled and put into the format of Power Point slides or handouts, the presentation should be rehearsed and tested. The test audience for this module should include both employees who are familiar with the computer incident response process and people who are not familiar with the process. This mix of test audiences allows training developers to test the accuracy and clarity of the material and whether or not the presentation is understandable by those who are not familiar with the process.

The key thing to test this module for is how well it explains how the computer incident response process works. The evaluators should be asked to answer the following questions:

1.   How well does the presentation explain each step in the alert process?

2.   Did you understand all of the material? (If no, then seek clarification on what was not understandable.)

3.   Does the material inspire you to help the organization when there is an alert?

4.   Was the material too technical?

5.   What part of the presentation did you like the most?

6.   Which slide or graphic did you like the most?

7.   What part of the presentation did you like the least?

8.   Which slide or graphic did you like the least?

9.   Should anything be added to the presentation?

10.   Should anything be taken out of the presentation?

8.8 Performing the Administrative Aspects of a Training Program

A specialized training department often handles the administrative aspects of training programs in large organizations. In some organizations the training function is a subpart of the human resources department. Regardless of how your organization is structured, there are several administrative aspects of a training program that must be managed, including:

- Scheduling training sessions
- Recruiting and training trainers
- Identifying which employee needs training
- Enrolling employees in training sessions
- Maintaining records of the employees who have attended training
- Scheduling employees for appropriate refresher courses
- Arranging for a training facility
- Reproducing and distributing training materials
- Analyzing the results of course evaluations done by participants

In most organizations one person could perform most of these functions on a part time basis. In larger and geographically dispersed organizations it may take several people to perform the various functions. If there is a training department in your organization it is advisable to work with them to manage or find people to manage the necessary training functions. If there is not a training department to work with, then a coordinator from the human resources department or the IT department could handle much of the work that needs to be done.

8.9   Action Steps to Improve Physical IT Security

The material in this chapter shows how to develop and implement training programs for physical IT security. As steps are taken to improve physical security of IT assets, managers, planners, and technical staff should understand the following principles:

- Education, training, and awareness are all necessary for the successful implementation of any information security program.
- Training for IT and security professionals is essential to effectively implement a physical IT security program.

- The key thing to remember when developing training programs is that the tone and the style of the training program should be good for the organization.

- Training modules should be evaluated and rehearsed before they are used organizationwide.

- Regardless of how your organization is structured, there are several administrative aspects of a training program that must be managed.

There are several steps that organizations can take to help improve the physical security of IT assets. Recommended steps are included at the end of each chapter. The action steps listed in Table 8.4 are designed to help an organization develop and implement training programs.

Table 8.4   *Action Steps to Improve Physical IT Security*

Step Number	Action Step
8.01	Evaluate the training needs for your IT and security professionals and recommend training programs and certification levels appropriate for your organization.
8.02	Establish a subgroup of the physical IT security working group to lead an effort to develop an organizationwide training program.
8.03	Establish a project schedule for the development and testing of the training material.
8.04	Develop a basic awareness training program that can be used as an introduction to an in-depth physical security training program or as a module in other training efforts in addition to a stand-alone seminar that can be used to promote awareness.
8.05	Develop and test all of your training modules and make modifications based on evaluator input.
8.06	Designate an HR staff person to coordinate the record keeping process for employees who have participated in the training.
8.07	Initiate the training process.
8.08	After several training sessions have taken place, evaluate the response to the training and determine if any changes should be made to the material or the process.

The Future of Physical Security for IT Assets

On April 26, 2004, Department of Homeland Security (DHS) Deputy Secretary James Loy spoke at the Kent State Symposium on Democracy. In his opening remarks he said, "What will that future look like? We began to understand on September 11, 2001. That morning, we passed into a far more menacing frontier of warfare, with the potential for far more horrifying consequences. International terrorism had become 'the new totalitarian threat.' While terrorism is not a new phenomenon, we must recognize that in the twenty-first century it is different, fundamentally different. It is not the localized terrorism of Ireland or even the Middle East. It is something very different and something much more sinister. We are only beginning to learn about it." Loy outlined some of the steps the government will be taking to improve homeland security in the near term, including:

- First, we will improve our information sharing and infrastructure protection, namely by improving partnerships within the government and with the private sector to strengthen vertical communication systems and significantly increase permanent protections around our nation's most vital assets.

- Second, many of us know that part of the tragedy of September 11th was that equipment didn't work across jurisdictions and disciplines. Fire department radios couldn't transmit to police department radios and the couplings that attach hoses to hydrants simply weren't compatible—even between nearby neighborhoods.

- And so, we must work together to establish truly interoperable communications and equipment—to give first responders the tools to do their jobs—in a way that replaces outdated, outmoded relics with an innovative and integrated system.

- Next, we'll broaden and enhance the security measures on our borders and at our ports, by expanding US-VISIT, FAST Lanes, and CSI, all the while continuing to facilitate the free flow of legitimate goods and people.

- Just as important as local governments and private companies are citizens. So, over the next year, Homeland Security will focus its efforts on raising the baseline level of preparedness across the nation, through new programs such as Ready for Business and Ready for Schools.

- In addition, we will be working to improve the service we provide to immigrants and visitors to our country and continue our quest to build the Department of Homeland Security as a model cabinet agency for the twenty-first century.

- Finally, we operate every day with the knowledge that our enemies are changing based on how we change. As we shore up one vulnerability, they work to uncover another. This is why science and technology is key to winning this new kind of war.

Like it or not, terrorism and homeland security countermeasures to terrorism are here to stay. This chapter explores what homeland security efforts may mean to security planners, managers, and staff, including the impact of national security plans and the role of Information Sharing and Analysis Centers (ISACS).

9.1   The Impact of National Security Plans

The National Strategy for the Physical Protection of Critical Infrastructures and Key Assets is the product of many months of consultation between a broad range of public sector and private sector organizations and leaders. This included extensive input from the federal departments and agencies, state and municipal government, private sector infrastructure owners and operators, the scientific and technology community, professional associations, research institutes, and concerned citizens across the country. This document is considered to represent the basis of national strategy.

The national strategy establishes a foundation for building and fostering the cooperative environment in which government, industry, and private citizens can carry out their respective protection responsibilities more effectively and efficiently. The strategic objectives that underpin the national critical infrastructure and key asset protection effort include:

- Identifying and ensuring the protection of those infrastructures and assets that we deem most critical in terms of national-level public health and safety, governance, economic and national security, and public confidence consequences

- Providing timely warning and ensuring the protection of those infrastructures and assets that face a specific, imminent threat

- Ensuring the protection of other infrastructures and assets that may become terrorist targets over time by pursuing specific initiatives and enabling a collaborative environment in which federal, state, and local governments and the private sector can better protect the infrastructures and assets they control

The facilities, systems, and functions that comprise the critical infrastructures are highly sophisticated and complex. They include human assets and physical and cyber systems that work together in processes that are highly interdependent. They also consist of key nodes that, in turn, are essential to the operation of the critical infrastructures in which they function.

Key assets and high-profile events are individual targets that, if attacked—in the worst-case scenarios—could result in not only large-scale human casualties and property destruction, but also profound damage to national prestige, morale, and confidence. Individually, key assets such as nuclear power plants and dams may not be vital to the continuity of critical services at the national level. However, a successful strike against such targets may result in a significant loss of life and property in addition to long-term, adverse public health and safety consequences.

Other key assets are symbolically equated with traditional values and institutions or political and economic power. National icons, monuments, and historical attractions preserve history, honor achievements, and represent the natural grandeur of the country. They celebrate ideals and a way of life and present attractive targets for terrorists, particularly when coupled with high-profile events and celebratory activities that bring together significant numbers of people. Enhancing countermeasures for any one terrorist tactic or target, therefore, makes it more likely that terrorists will favor another. Those targets could be your facility.

The national strategy assumes that terrorists' pursuit of their long term strategic objectives includes attacks on critical infrastructures and key assets. Terrorists target critical infrastructures to achieve three general types of effects:

Direct infrastructure effects: Cascading disruption or arrest of the functions of critical infrastructures or key assets through direct attacks on a critical node, system, or function

Indirect infrastructure effects: Cascading disruption and financial consequences for government, society, and economy through public and private sector reactions to an attack

Exploitation of infrastructure: Exploitation of elements of a particular infrastructure to disrupt or destroy another target

The national strategy documents state that the lion's share of critical infrastructures and key assets are owned and operated by the private sector. Customarily, private sector firms prudently engage in risk management planning and invest in security as a necessary function of business operations and customer confidence.

Moreover, in the present threat environment, the private sector generally remains the first line of defense for its own facilities. Consequently, private

Table 9.1   *Critical Infrastructure Sectors and Key Assets*

Critical Infrastructure Sectors	Key Assets
Agriculture and Food: 1,912,000 farms, 87,000 food-processing plants Water: 1,800 federal reservoirs, 1,600 municipal waste water facilities Public Health: 5,800 registered hospitals Emergency Services: 87,000 localities	National Monuments: 5,800 historic buildings and Icons
Defense Industrial Base: 250,000 firms in 215 distinct industries	Nuclear Power Plants: 104 commercial nuclear power plants
Telecommunications: 2 billion miles of cable	Dams: 80,000 dams
Energy	Government Facilities: 3,000 government owned/operated facilities
Electricity: 2,800 power plants	Commercial Assets: 460 skyscrapers
Oil and Natural Gas: 300,000 producing sites	
Transportation	

Table 9.1 *Critical Infrastructure Sectors and Key Assets (continued)*

Critical Infrastructure Sectors	Key Assets
Aviation: 5,000 public airports	
Railroads: 120,000 miles of major railroads	
Highways, Trucking: 590,000 highway and busing bridges	
Pipelines: 2 million miles of pipelines	
Maritime: 300 inland/costal ports	
Mass Transit: 500 major urban public transit operators	
Banking and Finance: 26,600 FDIC insured institutions	
Chemical Industry and Hazardous Materials: 66,000 chemical plants	
Postal and Shipping: 137 million delivery sites	

sector owners and operators should reassess and adjust their planning, insurance, and investment programs to better accommodate the increased risk presented by deliberate acts of violence. The national strategy identifies the critical infrastructure sectors and key assets shown in Table 9.1.

There are several types of threats that concern DHS and other government agencies. The potential damage that these new threats can cause is way beyond what most organizations have had to prepare to defend against in the past. The United States General Accounting Office (GAO) summarizes these threats as follows:

- Chemical weapons that are extremely lethal and capable of producing tens of thousands of casualties. They are also relatively easy to manufacture, using basic equipment, trained personnel, and precursor materials that often have legitimate dual uses.

- Biological weapons, which release large quantities of living, disease-causing microorganisms, have extraordinary lethal potential. Like chemical weapons, biological weapons are relatively easy to manufacture, requiring straightforward technical skills, basic equipment, and a seed stock of pathogenic microorganisms. Biological weapons are especially dangerous because we may not know immediately that we have been attacked, allowing an infectious agent time to spread. Moreover, biological agents can serve as a means of attack against humans as well as livestock and crops, inflicting casualties as well as economic damage.

- Radiological weapons, or "dirty bombs," combine radioactive material with conventional explosives. The individuals and groups engaged in terrorist activity can cause widespread disruption and fear, particularly in heavily populated areas.

- Nuclear weapons have enormous destructive potential. Terrorists who seek to develop a nuclear weapon must overcome two formidable challenges. First, acquiring or refining a sufficient quantity of material is very difficult—though not impossible. Second, manufacturing a workable weapon requires a very high degree of technical capability—though terrorists could feasibly assemble the simplest type of nuclear device. To get around these significant though not insurmountable challenges, terrorists could seek to steal or purchase a nuclear weapon.

- Terrorists, both domestic and international, continue to use traditional methods of violence and destruction to inflict harm and spread fear. They have used knives, guns, and bombs to kill the innocent. They have taken hostages and spread propaganda. Given the low expense, ready availability of materials, and relatively high chance for successful execution, terrorists will continue to make use of conventional attacks.

Table 9.1 illustrates the quantity of nodes, or points that need protection. The enormity of the security needs is rather mind-boggling. The only way to address needs of this magnitude is to try to move forward in an organized fashion and improving capabilities along the way. In the first twenty months of its existence DHS accomplished numerous things, including:

- DHS released a technical Statement of Requirements document for future communications interoperability (posted at www. SafecomProgram.gov) which has prompted significant private sector response and proposals for compatible solutions.

- DHS issued new standards for major pieces of first responder equipment, including personal air filtration protection, personal protective clothing for personnel working in contaminated areas, and basic protective clothing for law enforcement for incidents involving possible chemical, biological, or radiological incidents.

- The National Response Plan (NRP) was issued for public review. The NRP is designed to reflect the policy established in the Homeland Security Act of 2002, and Homeland Security Presidential Directive (HSPD)-5 to create a single comprehensive approach to domestic incident management. In HSPD-5, the president directed the development of an NRP to integrate federal domestic prevention, preparedness, response, and recovery plans into one all-discipline, all-hazards plan.

- DHS led the federal, state, local, and tribal development and completion of the National Incident Management System (NIMS). NIMS is based in large part on the incident command system taught by the United States Fire Administration and has been tested for some time by first responders throughout the country. NIMS is significant because it ensures that all of the nation's first responders are working under the same plan, using the same nomenclature, and are receiving consistent training. NIMS embraces the Incident Command System (ICS) and establishes a response structure that is scalable to meet the needs and complexity of a disaster event. In addition, a new organization was established—the NIMS Integration Center (NIC)—to ensure successful interagency coordination and implementation of the NIMS.

- DHS launched the Homeland Security Information Network (HSIN). The HSIN provides for real-time information to be shared between state and local agencies and the Homeland Security Operations Center (HSOC). Each state and major urban area's Homeland Security Advisor or other designated points of contact will receive software licenses, technology, and training to provide better efficiency, flow of information, and reduced vulnerabilities between federal and state homeland security professionals.

- The National Exercise Program was launched. Homeland Security Presidential Directive (HSPD)-8 outlines actions to strengthen and measure homeland security capabilities. The National Exercise Program has been identified as a priority initiative under HSPD-8 and initiated by the Department. The National Exercise Program establishes the framework for exercise scheduling, design, and evaluation for the exercises that are designed to test the response capabilities of the federal government and its state, local, and tribal partners. Efforts are made to include international and/or private sector participation. The cornerstone of the national performance-based exercise program is the Top Officials (TOPOFF) National Exercise Series, a biennial program that includes a functional exercise in year one and a full-scale exercise in year two, with continuity provided by a series of seminars.

- DHS launched the Transit and Rail Inspection Pilot Program (TRIP) to measure the feasibility of explosives screening for people and bags traveling on trains in the United States.

- DHS launched the National Emergency Management Baseline Capability Assessment Program (NEMB-CAP). Under this program, DHS is striving to complete evaluations of 56 state and state-level emergency management programs by the end of 2005. The NEMB-CAP involves a multi-year effort to assess, analyze, evaluate, and collectively frame state emergency management capabilities against a common national set of criteria.

- DHS awarded $79 million for communication interoperability pilot projects in 17 communities. The grants were awarded on a competitive basis in FY 2003. Results from these projects will be featured as best practices, and serve as models for other communities working to resolve this critical problem.

- DHS has provided states and localities with over $8.2 billion in State Homeland Security Grants for the purchase of specialized equipment to enhance the capability of state and local agencies to prevent and respond to incidents of terrorism involving the use of chemical, biological, radiological, nuclear, or explosive (CBRNE) weapons; for the protection of critical infrastructure and prevention of terrorist incidents; for the development, conduct, and evaluation of state CBRNE exercises and training programs; and for costs associated with updating and implementing each states' Homeland Security Strategy.

- The Urban Area Security Initiative (UASI) has provided a total of $1.4 billion to address the unique equipment, training, planning, and exercise needs of large, high-threat urban areas, and to assist them in building an enhanced and sustainable capacity to prevent, respond to, and recover from threats or acts of terrorism.

- Port security grants have funded risk assessments, command facilities, and other projects that will help local officials foil terrorism and contribute to laying the foundation for ports to continually make improvements and to employ new security technologies. In three rounds of port security grants, $441 million has been distributed.

- DHS disbursed $180 million in Emergency Management Performance Grants (EMPG) in FY 2004 to enable state and local governments to hire personnel and focus on an all-hazard approach to emergency management: preparedness, mitigation, response, and recovery. This was a 9% increase over FY 2003 and a 54% increase over historic levels (FY 2002 and earlier).

- By the end of FY 2004, $2 billion will have been distributed to more than 20,000 local fire departments through the Assistance to Fire Fighters Grant program. In FY 2004, $750 million will be awarded to thousands of fire departments across America to meet their preparedness needs.

- DHS has trained over 128,000 emergency responders in courses ranging from awareness and prevention to chemical HAZMAT techniques (473,000 from more than 5,000 jurisdictions since 1998). Through a partnership with Texas A&M University, a blended learning strategy was expedited to reach more emergency responders more quickly. Enrollment in FEMA's Independent Study Program, a web-based training and distance learning course for the nation's emergency managers and first responders, has increased to 187,520 in FY 2003, a 125% increase over 2001. Homeland Security trained a record number of leaders from volunteer fire departments.

- DHS launched the Strategic Communications Resources Effort (SECURE) Project. The department has installed secure videoconference capabilities, and secure phones and fax in the emergency operations centers of all 50 states and the District of Columbia. In addition, each state governor's office received a secure phone that allows states to transmit and receive classified information. In addition, the Department awarded $81 million in Emergency Operations Center (EOC) grants to those states that best demonstrated the need for the funding to reduce vulnerabilities and risk.

- DHS has worked on the National Urban Search and Rescue System (USAR). There are 28 USAR task forces that have acquired the training and equipment necessary to perform search and rescue in weapons of mass destruction (WMD) events.

- DHS organized the National Disaster Medical System (NDMS). These teams of medical professionals can be activated and pre-positioned during a disaster, thus ensuring faster response time and closer cooperation between these specialized teams and other teams providing direct aid to disaster victims.

- The Maritime Safety and Security Teams (MSSTs) were developed. Thirteen specialized units are in place to provide a rapid, deployable force to meet the nation's most serious port security threats. MSSTs provide a robust mix of maritime interdiction, law enforcement, and antiterrorism expertise focusing on threats to critical waterfront facilities, high-interest vessels, cruise ships, high-value military units, and major marine events.

- The joint BioWatch program was established. This sensor system is operated as a joint program with the Centers for Disease Control and the Environmental Protection Agency, in conjunction with the FBI. The program, which has been successfully operating in more than 30 of the nation's urban centers since early 2003, helps to quickly detect trace amounts of airborne pathogens such as anthrax in time to take protective actions, such as distributing life-saving pharmaceuticals. Since its beginning, the system has performed over a million tests with no false positives and only one true positive that was determined not be an act of terrorism, but came from an environmental source.

- The Countermeasures Test Bed was established as a field test bed in the New York/New Jersey region for evaluating new and existing security-related countermeasures in urban transportation venues, thereby facilitating their rapid transition to federal, state and local operational end-users. DHS has established field test sites in seaports, airports, highways, and rail facilities. In these sites, new countermeasure technology is tested for its effectiveness in the hands of front-line law enforcement personnel and other first responders.

- In February 2003, DHS launched the Ready Campaign (www. Ready.gov), a national public service advertising campaign designed to educate and empower American citizens to prepare for and respond to potential terrorist attacks and other emergencies. In December 2003, Homeland Security launched the Listo Campaign (www.Listo. gov), the Spanish-language version of Homeland Security's Ready Campaign. Extensions of the campaign, Ready for Business and Ready for Kids, will be launched by the end of the year.

- The launch of Citizen Corps, which is a component of USA Freedom Corps, provides opportunities for individuals to volunteer to help their communities prepare for and respond to emergencies by bringing together local leaders, citizen volunteers, and a network of first responder organizations. Their goal is to have all citizens participate in making their communities safer, stronger, and better prepared for preventing and handling threats of terrorism, crime, and disasters of all kinds.

In April 2004, the DHS's Science and Technology Directorate established the Homeland Security Institute, which is the Department's first government think tank or Federally Funded Research and Development Center (FFRDC). The Institute, managed by Analytic Services Incorporated (ANSER), will provide independent analysis on a variety of issues related to defense of the homeland. This FFRDC will particularly focus on those matters involving policy and security that scientific, technical, and analytical expertise, such as those in the extremely complex threat and vulnerability assessment areas.

The Homeland Security Act of 2002, Section 312, mandated the establishment of an FFRDC to provide Homeland Security access to an independent resource that could analyze and assess homeland security issues as they relate to critical analysis and decision support, mitigating homeland security threats, vulnerabilities, and risks while continually enhancing operational effectiveness.

The Homeland Security Institute will provide a dedicated, high-quality technical and analytical support capability aimed at helping Homeland Security set priorities and guide investments. The Institute will maintain an integrated systems approach to its mission by engaging in the following activities.

- Systems Evaluations: Systems evaluations will provide analyses that support homeland security program planning and execution. These analyses will cover all stages of development and deployment: initiation and conduct of research; development of technology; testing, evaluating, building and/or acquiring, deploying, and using systems. Included are systems analyses, risk analyses, vulnerability analyses, and the creation of strategic technology development plans to reduce vulnerabilities in the nation's critical infrastructure and key resources.

- Operational Assessments: Operational assessments will relate to systems development, operational performance, and homeland security strategy while providing a basis for revising operational concepts and mission needs. Included are evaluation of the effectiveness of measures deployed to enhance security of institutions and infrastructure; design and use of metrics to evaluate the effectiveness of Homeland Security programs; and design and support for exercises and simulations.

■ Technology Assessments: Technology assessments will provide scientific, technical, and analytical support for the identification, evaluation, and use of advanced technologies for homeland security systems. Assistance will be provided to Homeland Security and to other agencies and departments by evaluating the effectiveness of technologies under development and assessing their appropriateness for deployment.

■ Resource and Support Analyses: Resource and support efforts will develop methods, techniques, and tools (e.g., models) and conduct analyses that will lead to improved means for addressing resource issues, including investment decisions and cost implications of pending decisions. Included will be the economic and policy analyses to assess the distributed costs and benefits of alternative approaches to enhancing security.

■ Analyses Supporting the SAFETY Act: The SAFETY Act analyses will provide analytical and technical evaluations that can be used to support DHS determinations about candidate technologies.

■ Field Operations Analyses: The Institute may be required to provide small numbers of personnel to field activities to provide objective operations analyses, systems evaluations, and other technical and analytic support.

9.2   The Role of ISACS

The GAO has also conducted analysis of the information sharing efforts that the government feels are essential in fighting terrorism. Central to these efforts is the Information Analysis and Infrastructure Protection Directorate (IAIP), which is responsible for accessing, receiving, and analyzing law enforcement information, intelligence information, and other threat and incident information from respective agencies of federal, state, and local governments and the private sector. The IAIP also takes the lead in combining and analyzing such information to identify and assess the nature and scope of terrorist threats. IAIP is also tasked with coordinating with other federal agencies to administer the Homeland Security Advisory System to provide specific warning information along with advice on appropriate protective measures and countermeasures.

Further, IAIP is responsible for disseminating, as appropriate, information analyzed by DHS within the department, to other federal agencies, to state and local government agencies, and to private sector entities.

The Homeland Security Act of 2002 makes DHS and its IAIP directorate also responsible for key critical infrastructure protection (CIP) functions for the federal government. CIP involves activities that enhance the security of our nation's cyber and physical public and private infrastructure that are critical to national security, national economic security, and/or national public health and safety. Information sharing is a key element of these activities.

As part of its CIP responsibilities, IAIP is responsible for developing a comprehensive national plan for securing the key resources and critical infrastructure of the United States. The IAIP is also supposed to recommend measures to protect the key resources and critical infrastructure of the United States in coordination with other federal agencies and in cooperation with state and local government agencies and authorities, the private sector, and other entities.

Federal CIP policy has continued to evolve since the mid-1990s through a variety of working groups, special reports, executive orders, strategies, and organizations. In particular, Presidential Decision Directive 63 (PDD 63) issued in 1998 established CIP as a national goal and described a strategy for cooperative efforts by government and the private sector to protect the physical and cyber-based systems essential to the minimum operations of the economy and the government. To accomplish its goals, PDD 63 established and designated organizations to provide central coordination and support.

PDD 63 addressed the protection of the critical sectors listed in Table 9.1. In the Clinton administration view, the elimination of potential vulnerabilities requires a cooperative and coordinated effort of the public and the private sectors. This philosophy led to the creation of industry-specific Information Sharing and Analysis Centers (ISACs).

The structure and functions of the ISACs and their relationship to the government was determined by consulting with private sector organizations and with assistance from sector related federal government agencies. PDD 63 called for an action plan on the ISACs within 180 days of date the directive was issued. The value of the ISAC approach is found in the ability to acquire and share information with the group in a way that individual group members cannot accomplish. This process often involves the rapid assessment and conversion of information that individual ISAC members had held as proprietary and confidential into a form that can be shared both with ISAC members and with other affected or interested parties.

In spite of progress made in establishing ISACs, additional efforts are needed. All sectors do not have a fully established ISAC, and even for those sectors that do, our recent work showed that participation may be mixed, and the amount of information being shared between the federal government and private sector organizations varies. The author visited the websites of several ISACs to collect information about their mission statements, membership, and benefits. The summaries compiled for this chapter support the findings of the GAO regarding the uneven maturity of the ISACs.

The mission of the Information Sharing and Analysis Centers Council (ISAC Council) is to advance the physical and cyber security of the critical infrastructures of North America by establishing and maintaining a framework for valuable interaction between and among the ISACs and with government. Eleven ISACs are members of the ISAC Council:

- Chemical Industry ISAC (chemicalisac.chemtrec.com)

- Electricity Sector ISAC (www.esisac.com)

- Energy ISAC (www.energyisac.com)

- Financial Services ISAC (www.fsisac.com)

- Healthcare ISAC (www.hcisac.org)

- Highway ISAC (www.trucking.org/insideata/isac)

- Information Technology ISAC (www.it-isac.org)

- National Coordinating Center for Telecommunications ISAC (www.ncs.gov/ncc/main.html)

- Public Transit ISAC (www.apta.com)

- Surface Transportation ISAC (surfacetransportationisac.org)

- Water ISAC (www.waterisac.org)

Several ISACs are not members of the ISAC Council, including the Aviation ISAC headed by the Airports Council International-North America (ACI-NA). The ACI-NA represents local, regional, and state governing bodies that own and operate commercial airports in the United States and Canada. ACI-NA member airports enplane more than 98% of the domestic and virtually all the international airline passenger and cargo traffic in North America. Over 300 aviation-related businesses are also members of the association, which is the largest of the six worldwide regions of Airports Council International. The ACI-NA website offers lots of information, but it is not clear which part of that information is actually intended to support the ISAC mission (www.aci-na.org).

The Interstate ISAC, which was established by the National Association of State Chief Information Officers (NASCIO), is also not a member of the ISAC Council. The Interstate ISAC provides a mechanism for informing state officials about DHS threat warnings, alerts, and other relevant information, and for state officials to report information to DHS. A visit to the Interstate ISAC's website provides very little information as to their level of activity as an ISAC (www.nascio.org).

9.2.1 The Chemical Sector ISAC

The website established by the Chemical Sector ISAC states that CHEMTREC® and other elements of the American Chemistry Council have worked closely with DHS and the FBI to assist law enforcement and intelligence agencies (chemicalisac.chemtrec.com). The primary goal of the Chemical Sector ISAC is to enable DHS to disseminate timely and actionable assessment, advisories, and alerts to appropriate government and private sector entities when such incidents are deemed to have possible serious national security, economic, or social consequences.

The Chemical Sector ISAC is intended for those companies or other organizations involved in the production, storage, transportation, and delivery of chemicals. Participation by the chemical industry is intended to be inclusive to maximize the value and utility of the ISAC.

The Chemical Sector ISAC utilizes CHEMTREC, the chemical industry's 24-hour emergency communication center as the communication link between the DHS and ISAC participants. When CHEMTREC receives information from the DHS, that information is immediately transmitted, on an around-the-clock basis, to Chemical Sector ISAC participants utilizing electronic mail and a secure website. The Chemical Sector ISAC includes the following key elements:

- A 24 hour, electronic communication network to provide chemical facilities and chemical transportation systems with timely, accurate, and actionable warnings for both physical and cyber (computer related) threats

- An electronic communication system that will allow for voluntary and secure electronic reporting to DHS of malicious, unexplained, or suspicious incidents involving chemical facilities or chemicals in commerce to allow federal intelligence and law enforcement agencies to identify and analyze incidents

9.2.2　The Electricity Sector ISAC

The website established by for the ES-ISAC (www.esisac.com) states that the ISAC facilitates communications between electric sector participants, federal government, and other critical infrastructure industries. The North American Electric Reliability Council (NERC) operates the Information Sharing and Analysis Center for the Electricity Sector (ES-ISAC). The ES-ISAC disseminates threat indications, analyses, and warnings, together with interpretations, to assist electricity sector participants take protective actions.

The following publications are available from the ES-ISAC website:

- DOE Vulnerability Assessment Methodology (VAS) (September 2002)
- DOE VAS Overview (September 2001)
- DOE Vulnerability Survey Checklist (February 2002)
- DOE Vulnerability Survey Checklist, Small and Medium Facilities (August 2002)
- DOE VAS Lessons Learned, Best Practices (September 2001)
- Cyber Security Standard (August 2003)
- Cyber Security Standard Implementation Plan (August 2003)
- Threat Alert System and Physical Response Guidelines for the Electricity Sector Version 2.0 (October 2002)
- Threat Alert System and Cyber Response Guidelines for the Electricity Sector Version 2.0 (October 2002)
- Security Guidelines for the Electricity Sector: Version 1.0 (June 2002):
  - Guideline Overview
  - Vulnerability and Risk Assessment
  - Emergency Plans
  - Continuity of Business Practices
  - Communications
  - Physical Security
  - Cyber Security: Risk Management
  - Cyber Security: Access Controls
  - Cyber Security: IT Firewalls

- Cyber Security: Intrusion Detection
- Employment Background Screening
- Protecting Potentially Sensitive Information
- Securing Remote Access to Electronic Control and Protection Systems
- Threat and Incident Reporting

9.2.3 The Energy ISAC

The Energy ISAC's website (www.energyisac.com) is exclusively for, and designed by, professionals in the energy industries. The Energy ISAC is a clearinghouse for information on threats, vulnerabilities, solutions, and best practices. This information is designed to help companies better understand the threats and vulnerabilities to their business so that they can take appropriate action. The Energy ISAC is operated by SAIC's Enterprise Security Solutions Group.

Members can submit information anonymously and receive near-real-time updates. The Energy ISAC data will be used to share incident information among members in near-real-time. The data is also used to develop trending and benchmarking information for the benefit of the members, and associations can use the information to develop needed standards, awareness programs, and legislation.

The Energy ISAC provides a near-real-time threat and warning capability to the energy industry on a 24×7 basis. It provides two-way sharing, so that reported incidents in the sector may be shared with other members in real time. The Energy ISAC provides energy companies with:

- A wide range of information on threats and vulnerabilities (physical, cyber-security, and interdependencies).
- Early notification of physical and cyber threats
- Possible responses to those threats (e.g., information technology solutions and patches, and physical and information security tips)
- Alert conditions
- Best practices
- A forum allowing members to communicate in a secure environment

Companies in the oil, natural gas, and electric power industries are eligible to join. Relevant energy activities include exploration, production, processing, transmission, distribution, transportation, storage, trading, supervisory control and data acquisition (SCADA), and e-commerce of energy commodities.

9.2.4 The Financial Sector ISAC

The website established by the Financial Services Information Sharing and Analysis Center (FS-ISAC, Inc.) provides considerably more information than those of other ISACs that are not tied to a larger organization. Formed as an industry initiative in 1999, the FS-ISAC is exclusively for, and designed by, professionals in the banking, securities, and insurance industries.

One of the initial goals of the FS-ISAC was to help member organizations prepare for Y2K by providing timely information on potential vulnerabilities while at the same time creating a forum for members to share their insights and experiences. In response to the events of the past few years, the growing threat of both physical and cyber attacks to the financial services sector, and the recommendations of HSPD-7, the role of the FS-ISAC has been restructured to serve all sector participants at a level that meets their needs.

By gathering reliable and timely information from financial services providers; commercial firms; federal, state, and local government agencies; law enforcement; and other trusted resources, the FS-ISAC is positioned to disseminate threat alerts and other critical information to your organization with analysis and recommended solutions from top industry experts.

Through the FS-ISAC restricted website, eligible firms may anonymously share information about security risks, vulnerabilities, and solutions. Certain membership levels allow participation in conference calls within hours of notification of crisis to minimize the damage to your organization and to the industry.

FS-ISAC membership is recommended by the U.S. Department of the Treasury, the Office of the Controller of the Currency, the Department of Homeland Security, the United States Secret Service, and the Financial Service Sector Coordinating Council, which represents financial services industry associations with over 27,000 members.

A new company, the FS-ISAC, Inc., was created to manage and offer memberships in the FS-ISAC. The FS-ISAC Board of Directors determines member eligibility, enforces member eligibility verification through trusted third parties, and oversees the operation of the FS-ISAC. The FS-ISAC is operated by SAIC's Enterprise Security Solutions Group.

Financial service providers are encouraged to take advantage of the first industrywide database of electronic security threats, vulnerabilities, incidents, and solutions. The FS-ISAC offers a confidential venue for sharing security vulnerabilities and solutions. It facilitates trust among its participants.

Members benefit from the FS-ISAC's unique proactive means of mitigating cyber security risks. The real value add is the participation in member meetings, tabletop exercises, bi-weekly threat calls, and crisis calls in which security professionals develop working relationships when bad things happen.

9.2.5 The Healthcare ISAC

The Healthcare Information Sharing and Analysis Center (HCISAC) website provides very little public information (www.hcisac.org). The website states that HCISAC serves as a first responder to such threats and provides a framework to achieve fundamental and vital cyber security objectives for the industry. The purpose of the HCISAC is to protect the components of the healthcare industry's cyber and physical infrastructure that are essential to patient care delivery.

The mission of the HCISAC is to gather, analyze, and disseminate to its members an integrated view of cyber and physical threats and vulnerabilities of the healthcare industry, in partnership with our national Homeland Security activities.

HCISAC members have access to information analyses derived from information provided by several sources, including other HCISAC members, the United States government and law enforcement agencies, technology providers and security associations, and from the private healthcare sector as a whole. Data collected are used to provide alerts and develop awareness and responses based on the state of the healthcare infrastructures and the national threat environment.

9.2.6 The Highway ISAC

The Highway ISAC is operated by American Trucking Associations (ATA). The ISAC part of the website (www.trucking.org/insideata/isac) is relatively small compared to the ATA parent site. The mission of the Highway ISAC is to "serve as an alert system, leveraging the Internet and other communication channels, to provide the highway sector with incident, threat, and vulnerability information."

ATA and other industry members have created this Anti-Terrorism Action Plan. Trucking industry representatives have established this security blueprint with a set of recommendations for a joint industry–government effort to evaluate and mitigate possible security risks to our industry in the near, medium, and long term.

The essential goals of ATA are to ensure that a truck or its cargo will not be used as a weapon of mass destruction and that the wheels of commerce continue to roll during a terrorist threat or even a terrorist attack. ATA activities include:

- Expansion of the Highway Watch program to include training professional truck drivers and truck stop employees to be the eyes and ears of America's trucking army and to report suspicious activity on the public roadways

- Evaluating technologies that could possibly assist the trucking industry to effectively improve the security of trucks, terminals, and other operations

- Improving industry access to information databases to undertake security and criminal background checks of commercial truck drivers and possibly other employees in sensitive positions

- Expanding a strong liaison program with relevant government agencies, law enforcement representatives, and our trucking industry counterparts and government agencies in Canada and Mexico

- Assessing vulnerabilities within trucking operations and providing access to educational and training programs that promote security risk management

9.2.7   The Information Technology ISAC

The IT-ISAC website (www.it-isac.org) states that because information technology is common to all national infrastructures, critical or otherwise, the model is a natural bridge between all the ISACs, taking a holistic approach to threat definitions and solutions. The IT-ISAC exists to enable members to share data. Using this shared data and other information, the ISAC operations staff gathers, analyzes, and disseminates to the members an integrated view of information system vulnerabilities, threats, and incidents that are relevant to the ISAC's sponsoring sector organization.

Other information may be gathered from public and private sources, including semi-private organizations such as CERT, DHS, or private organizations. The ultimate use of all of this data is to produce a coherent picture of the current state of the threat to the members. Likewise, the ISAC Operations also shares best security practices and solutions among its members. Overall, the IT-ISAC website provides little public information.

9.2.8 The Telecommunications ISAC

The National Coordinating Center for Telecommunications ISAC (www.ncs.gov/ncc/main.html) provides a considerable amount of information about the ISAC. A brief history statement indicates that in 1982 the telecommunications industry and federal government officials identified the need for a joint mechanism to coordinate initiation and restoration of national security and emergency preparedness (NS/EP) telecommunication services. In 1983 the group recommended to the National Security Telecommunications Advisory Committee (NSTAC) and to President Reagan that a joint industry-and-government-staffed NCC be created as a central organization to handle emergency telecommunication requests. On January 3, 1984, the NCC opened for business.

In January 2000, the National Coordinator for Security, Infrastructure Protection, and Counter-terrorism designated the National Coordinating Center for Telecommunications as the ISAC for telecommunications. On March 1, 2000, the NCC-ISAC commenced operations. The initial NCC-ISAC membership was based on NCC membership, which is evolving to reflect a broader base of technologies comprising the telecommunications infrastructure.

NCC-ISAC supports the mission assigned by Executive Order 12472 and the national critical infrastructure protection goals of government and industry. The NCC-ISAC facilitates voluntary collaboration and information sharing among its participants, gathering information on vulnerabilities, threats, intrusions, and anomalies from telecommunications industry, government, and other sources.

The NCC-ISAC analyzes the data with the goal of averting or mitigating effects on the telecommunications infrastructure. Additionally, data are used to establish baseline statistics and patterns and are maintained as a library of historical data. Results will be sanitized and disseminated in accordance with sharing agreements established for that purpose by the NCC-ISAC participants.

The North Atlantic Treaty Organization (NATO) Civil Communications Planning Committee (CCPC) is responsible for ensuring the continued availability of civil communications during crises and war, for civil and military purposes. The NCC has sponsored a Crisis Management Exercise for the CCPC that familiarized telecommunications experts on NATO's evolving mission and function, emergency planning committees, crisis management procedures, documentation, and crisis coordination.

During the period leading up to Y2K, the NCC successfully organized a collaborative partnership with the International Telecommunication Union (ITU). This working relationship enabled a more comprehensive picture of Y2K events and an effective warning capability. In November 1999, a demonstration of the NCC Y2K database to an ITU forum in London resulted in companies from 41 countries agreeing to share Y2K incident information using the database. This level of participation allowed the NCC to develop a comprehensive picture of Y2K-related events as the millennium unfolded, starting at the International Date Line.

The NCC all-hazard response relies on the flexible application of OMNCS resources to meet crises occurring primarily in NTMS Response Levels I and II. During Response Level III, the NCC will convene to perform functions similar to its Response Level II functions for as long as it is operationally capable, or as provisions of the OMNCS COOP apply.

The NCC Initial Response Team (IRT) will be the first NCS organization responding to any crisis. The IRT will conduct an initial assessment of the crisis and alert other NCC and OMNCS personnel, as necessary, to staff an EOT appropriately sized for the emergency. The flexibility of the EOT structure will allow seamless movement from an NCC IRT to NCC EOTs to support a response in any of the three NTMS Response Levels.

NTMS Response Level I is the lowest level of enhanced NTMS operations and defines day-to-day operations and response activities triggered by minor emergencies and disasters affecting the telecommunications infrastructure. Level I is in effect throughout a broad range of low-level emergencies or disasters, up to major disasters in which the Federal Response Plan (FRP) is not activated, and extraordinary situations, as declared by the director of the Federal Emergency Management Agency (FEMA). A Federal Emergency Communications Coordinator (FECC) may be involved during NTMS Response Level I situations.

The manager, NCC, and the NCC Telecommunications manager monitor crises and emergencies occurring within NTMS Response Level I to ensure that adequate national security/emergency preparedness (NS/EP) telecommunication services are being provided. To that end, the NCC coordinates with the telecommunications industry, government representatives, federal department and agency operations and watch centers, and the NCS regional manager or FECC (if deployed) as required.

Activation of NTMS Response Level II occurs concurrently with a national Emergency Support Function #2 (ESF #2) activation under FRP provisions. During Response Level II, FEMA activates elements to provide an initial response to the disaster or emergency. These elements perform an initial assessment of the severity and impact of the disaster, and provide information needed to determine requirements and identify the critical resources needed to support response activities. Some of these elements continue to provide emergency response throughout the entire disaster.

The FRP elements activated in conjunction with an ESF #2 activation, and the corresponding NTMS Level II Response, include the Catastrophic Disaster Response Group (CDRG), the Advance Element of the Emergency Response Team (ERT-A), Ground Assessment Task Force (Task Force), and the Emergency Response Team (ERT). Specific ESF #2 elements activated include an FECC, Emergency Communications Staff (ECS), NCC, NCS DALO, NCS representative to the CDRG, and the ESF #2 representative to the Emergency Support Team (EST). The manager, NCS, the director, OSTP, and, if required, the Joint Telecommunications Resources Board (JTRB) monitor the disaster response.

An activation of NTMS Response Level III will occur in anticipation of a national security emergency or concurrently with presidential activation of the federal national security structure. During Response Level III, staff assigned to the National Emergency Management Team (NEMT) Communications Functional Group (CFG), the NCC, multiple Regional Emergency Management Team (REMT) CFGs, and government and industry NTMS Operating Centers (OCs) will move to predetermined locations and prepare to respond to the threat. Postmovement activities will include reviewing applicable operations plans; performing communications checks between the NEMT, the NCC, the REMTs, and the OCs; reporting readiness status; and coordinating with other functional groups within the NEMT and REMTs. After an attack has occurred, these elements will perform an initial assessment of the severity and impact of the attack, provide information to determine requirements for critical resources needed to support response activities, and take actions to restore and reconstitute the nation's telecommunications infrastructure. An explanation of the elements activated in Response Level III, their interaction with other elements, the functions they perform, and their communications and information management requirements are detailed on the website.

During Response Level III operations, the NCC will continue to perform functions similar to its Response Level II functions for as long as it is operationally capable, or if the provisions of the OMNCS COOP apply. Additionally, the NCC will directly support the NEMT CFG and the director, OSTP, in the formulation of national telecommunications policy and guidance, and provide a conduit for the execution of that policy through its government and industry representatives.

9.2.9 The Public Transit ISAC

APTA established a public transportation Information Sharing and Analysis Center (Public Transit ISAC) where industry members can share security information, especially about evolving terrorist threats or ongoing information system attacks. FTA provided the initial funding of the ISAC. The Public Transit ISAC website is co-mingled with the APTA website (www.apta.com) and the Surface Transportation ISAC (surfacetransportationisac.org).

In early 2002, the Federal Transit Administrator (FTA) began conducting security readiness assessments of the largest, highest-risk transit agencies. It was quickly concluded that transit systems need timely and transit-specific threat information and intelligence analysis. On January 23, 2003, the American Public Transit Association formed a partnership to protect the public transportation infrastructure.

APTA is a nonprofit international association of over 1,500 public and private member organizations, including transit systems and commuter rail operators; planning, design, construction, and finance firms; product and service providers; academic institutions; and transit associations and state departments of transportation. APTA members serve the public interest by providing safe, efficient, and economical transit services and products.

The Department of Transportation and APTA sponsored a series of workshops to help raise awareness of both physical and information-based threats and vulnerabilities to the nation's public transportation industry, and begin to develop strategies to address those threats. The main message was that with the potential threat of terrorist attack; cooperation and coordination among all aspects of public transportation, the federal government, and law enforcement; and rapid dissemination of threat information is vital both to the nation's security and its economic well-being.

The ISAC works closely with ISACs established for other critical sectors, such as banking and finance and telecommunications, as well as with the

National Infrastructure Protection Center. Besides the existing Surface Transportation ISAC, there currently is one other transportation ISAC: the aviation ISAC headed by the Airports Council International-North America.

9.2.10 The Water ISAC

The Water ISAC website (www.waterisac.org) provides a fair amount of information about the activities of the ISAC. The website states that the Water ISAC is a highly secure Internet portal that provides the best source for sensitive security information and alerts to help America's drinking water and waste water community protect consumers and the environment.

The Water ISAC's information and tools can be used by water system managers and security personnel to assist in identifying and assessing threats, in taking measures to mitigate those threats, and in analyzing incident reports. It also serves as an important link between the water sector and federal environmental, homeland security, law enforcement, intelligence, and public health agencies.

In addition, the Water ISAC provides resources to help utilities complete and continually improve their vulnerability assessments and emergency response plans, required by law for many systems. The products and services offered on the website include:

- Alerts on potential terrorist activity

- Information on water security from federal homeland security, intelligence, law enforcement, public health, and environment agencies

- Databases of chemical, biological, and radiological agents

- Physical vulnerabilities and security solutions

- Notification of cyber vulnerabilities and technical fixes

- Research, reports, and other information

- A secure means for reporting security incidents

- Vulnerability assessment tools and resources

- Emergency preparedness and response resources

- Secure electronic bulletin boards and chat rooms on security topics

- Summaries of open-source security information

9.3   Action Steps to Improve Physical IT Security

The material in this chapter shows activities of DHS and the ISACs that may affect the physical IT security efforts of your organization at some time in the future. As steps are taken to improve physical security of IT assets, managers, planners, and technical staff should understand the following rudiments:

- The efforts to prevent terrorism may affect your approach to physical IT security.

- There are numerous sources of information that may help you improve security or understand new threats.

- Not all sources or information are equal, and the ISAC that serves your industry sector may not be as developed as the ISAC for other sectors.

There are several steps that organizations can take to help improve the physical security of IT assets. Recommended steps are included at the end of each chapter. The action steps listed in Table 9.2 are designed to help an organization determine what benefit it may be able to derive from information on threats, vulnerabilities, and trends from DHS or an ISAC.

Table 9.2   *Action Steps to Improve Physical IT Security*

Step Number	Action Step
9.01	Evaluate the impact of national security strategies on your operations and security plans. Make recommendations to management on how you can maximize the benefit you receive from those plans.
9.02	Evaluate the potential benefit of becoming a member of one or more of the ISACs. Make recommendations to management on how you can maximize the benefit you receive from those organizations.
9.03	Evaluate ways in which you can monitor the activities of government agencies such as DHS to determine if new activities or information from the agencies can help you improve your physical IT security. Make recommendations to management on how you can maximize the benefit you receive from monitoring those agencies.

Physical Computer Security Resources

Air Conditioning Contractors of America
www.acca.org

Air-Conditioning and Refrigeration Institute, Inc.
www.ari.org

Airport Consultants Council
www.acconline.org

Alliance for Fire & Smoke Containment & Control
www.afscconline.org

American Council of Engineering Companies (ACEC)
www.acec.org

American Institute of Architects (AIA), Security Resource Center
www.aia.org/security

American Institute of Chemical Engineers
www.aiche.org/ccpssecurity

American Lifelines Alliance
www.americanlifelinesalliance.org

American Planning Association
www.planning.org

American Portland Cement Alliance
www.portcement.org/apca

American Public Works Association
www.apwa.net

American Railway Engineering & Maintenance of Way Association
www.arema.org

American Society for Industrial Security International (ASIS)
www.asisonline.org

American Society of Civil Engineers (ASCE)
www.asce.org

American Society of Heating, Refrigerating, and Air-Conditioning Engineers
(ASHRAE)
www.ashrae.org

American Society of Interior Designers
www.asid.org

American Society of Landscape Architects (ASLA)
www.asla.org

American Society of Mechanical Engineers (ASME)
www.asme.org

American Underground Construction Association (AUA)
www.auca.org or www.auaonline.org

American Water Resources Association (AWRA)
www.awra.org

Anser Institute for Homeland Security (ANSER)
www.homelandsecurity.org

Applied Technology Council
www.atcouncil.org

Architectural Engineering Institute (AEI) of ASCE
www.asce.org

Associated General Contractors of America
www.agc.org

Associated Locksmiths of America
www.aloa.org

Association of Metropolitan Water Agencies
www.amwa.net

Association of State Dam Safety Officials
www.damsafety.org

Battelle Memorial Institute, National Security Program
www.battelle.org

Building Futures Council
www.thebfc.com

Building Performance Assessment Team
www.fema.gov/mit/bpat

Center for Strategic and International Studies (CSIS)
www.csis.org

Centers for Disease Control and Prevention (CDC), National Institute
for Occupational Safety and Health (NIOSH)
www.cdc.gov/niosh

Central Intelligence Agency (CIA)
www.cia.gov

Civil Engineering Research Foundation (CERF) of ASCE
www.cerf.org

Construction Industry Institute
www.construction-institute.org

Construction Industry Roundtable
www.cirt.org

Construction Innovation Forum
www.cif.org

Construction Specifications Institute
www.csinet.org

Construction Users Roundtable
www.curt.org

Council on Tall Buildings and Urban Habitat (CTBUH)
www.ctbuh.org

Defense Threat Reduction Agency (DTRA)
www.dtra.mil

Department of Commerce Critical Infrastructure Assurance Office (CIAO)
www.ciao.gov

Department of Energy (DOE)
www.energy.gov

Design-Build Institute of America
www.dbia.org

Federal Bureau of Investigation: Terrorism in the United States reports
www.fbi.gov/publications/terror/terroris.htm

Federal Emergency Management Agency (FEMA)
www.fema.gov

Federal Facilities Council (FFC) Standing Committee on Physical Security
and Hazard Mitigation
www.nationalacademies.org/ffc/Physical_Security_Hazard_Mitigation.html

Healthy Buildings International, Inc.
www.healthybuildings.com

Homeland Protection Institute, Ltd.
www.hpi-tech.org

Human Caused Hazards
www.fema.gov/hazards

Information Technology Association of America (ITAA)
www.itaa.org

Inland Rivers Ports and Terminals
www.irpt.net

Institute of Electrical and Electronics Engineers, Inc. - USA
www.ieeeusa.org

International Association of Emergency Managers (IAEM)
www.iaem.com

International Association of Foundation Drilling
www.adsc-iafd.com

International Code Council (ICC)
www.intlcode.org

International Facility Management Association (IFMA)
www.ifma.org

Mitigation Planning
www.fema.gov/fima/planning.shtm

Multidisciplinary Center for Earthquake Engineering Research
mceer.buffalo.edu

National Academy of Sciences
www4.nationalacademies.org/nas/nashome.nsf

National Center for Explosion Resistant Design
www.engineering.missouri.edu/explosion.htm

National Center for Manufacturing Sciences
www.ncms.org

National Concrete Masonry Association
www.ncma.org

National Conference of States on Building Codes and Standards
www.ncsbcs.org

National Council of Structural Engineers Associations (NCSEA)
www.ncsea.com

National Defense Industrial Association (NDIA)
www.ndia.org

National Emergency Managers Association (NEMA)
www.nemaweb.org

National Fire Protection Association
www.nfpa.org

National Institute of Building Sciences (NIBS)
www.nibs.org

National Institute of Justice (NIJ)
www.ojp.usdoj.gov/nij

National Institute of Standards and Technology (NIST),
Building and Fire Research Laboratory
www.bfrl.nist.gov

National Precast Concrete Association
www.precast.org

National Research Council
www.nationalacademies.org/nrc

North American Electric Reliability Council (NERC)
www.nerc.com

Office of Domestic Preparedness (ODP)
www.ojp.usdoj.gov/odp

Partnership for Critical Infrastructure (PCIS)
www.pcis.org

Portland Cement Association (PCA)
www.portcement.org

Primary Glass Manufacturers Council
www.primaryglass.org

Protective Glazing Council
www.protectiveglazing.org

Protective Technology Center at Penn State University
www.ptc.psu.edu

Public Entity Risk Institute
www.riskinstitute.org

SANS (SysAdmin, Audit, Network, Security) Institute
www.sans.org

Security Design Coalition
www.designingforsecurity.org

Security Industry Association (SIA)
www.siaonline.org/

Society of Fire Protection Engineers
www.sfpe.org

Structural Engineering Institute (SEI) of ASCE
www.seinstitute.org

Sustainable Buildings Industry Council
www.sbicouncil.org

The Infrastructure Security Partnership (TISP)
www.tisp.org

U.S. Chamber of Commerce, Center for Corporate Citizenship (CCC)
www.uschamber.com/ccc

U.S. Department of Justice
www.usdoj.gov

U.S. General Services Administration (GSA)
www.gsa.gov

U.S. Marshals Service (USMS)
www.usdoj.gov/marshals

Water and Wastewater Equipment Manufacturers Association
www.wwema.org

B

Physical Security Glossary and Acronyms

Glossary of Terms

Access control system: an electronic system that controls entry and egress from a building or area.

Access control: limiting access to information system resources to authorized users, programs, processes, or other systems only.

Accountability: explicit assignment of responsibilities for oversight of areas of control to executives, managers, staff, owners, providers, and users of minimum essential infrastructure resource elements.

Aggressor: any person seeking to compromise a function or structure.

Airborne contamination: chemical or biological agents introduced into and fouling the source of supply of breathing or conditioning air.

Alpha particles: alpha particles have a very short range in air and a very low ability to penetrate other materials, but also have a strong ability to ionize materials. Alpha particles are unable to penetrate even the thin layer of dead cells of human skin and consequently are not an external radiation hazard. Alpha-emitting nuclides inside the body as a result of inhalation or ingestion are a considerable internal radiation hazard.

Antiterrorism: defensive measures used to reduce the vulnerability of individuals, forces, and property to terrorist acts.

Area lighting: lighting that illuminates a large exterior area.

Assessment: evaluation and interpretation of measurements and other information to provide a basis for decision making.

Asset: a resource of value requiring protection. An asset can be tangible (people, buildings, facilities, equipment, activities, operations, and information) or intangible (processes, information, and reputation).

Beta particles: high-energy electrons emitted from the nucleus of an atom during radioactive decay. They normally can be stopped by the skin or a very thin sheet of metal.

Biochemicals: the chemicals that make up or are produced by living things.

Biological agents: living organisms or the materials derived from them that cause disease in or harm to humans, animals, or plants, or cause deterioration of material.

Biological warfare: the intentional use of biological agents as weapons to kill or injure humans, animals, or plants, or to damage equipment.

Blast-resistant glazing: window glazing that is resistant to blast effects because of the interrelated function of the frame and glazing material properties, frequently dependent upon tempered glass, polycarbonate, or laminated glazing.

Bollard: a vehicle barrier consisting of a cylinder, usually made of steel and sometimes filled with concrete, placed on end in the ground and spaced about 3 feet apart to prevent vehicles from passing, but allowing entrance of pedestrians and bicycles.

Building hardening: enhanced construction that reduces vulnerability to external blast and ballistic attacks.

Building separation: the distance between the closest points on the exterior walls of adjacent buildings or structures.

Casualty (toxic) agent: agents that produce incapacitation, serious injury, or death, and can be used to incapacitate or kill victims. They are the blister, blood, choking, and nerve agents.

Chemical agent: a chemical substance that is intended to kill, seriously injury, or incapacitate people through physiological effects.

Clear zone: an area that is clear of visual obstructions and landscape materials that could conceal a threat or perpetrator.

Closed circuit television (CCTV): an electronic system of cameras, control equipment, recorders, and related apparatus used for surveillance or alarm assessment.

Collateral damage: injury or damage to assets that are not the primary target of an attack.

Compromise: a breach of security policy involving unauthorized disclosure, modification, destruction, or loss of information, whether deliberate or unintentional.

Contamination: the undesirable deposition of a chemical, biological, or radiological material on the surface of structures, areas, objects, or people.

Continuity of services and operations: controls to ensure that, when unexpected events occur, departmental/agency minimum essential infrastructure services and operations continue.

Control center: a centrally located room or facility staffed by personnel charged with the oversight of specific situations and/or equipment.

Controlled area: an area into which access is controlled or limited. It is that portion of a restricted area usually near or surrounding a limited or exclusion area.

Controlled perimeter: a physical boundary at which vehicle and personnel access is controlled at the perimeter of a site. Access control at a controlled perimeter should demonstrate the capability to search individuals and vehicles.

Covert entry: attempts to enter a facility by using false credentials or stealth.

Crime Prevention Through Environmental Design (CPTED): a crime prevention strategy based on evidence that the design and form of the built environment can influence human behavior. CPTED usually involves the use of three principles: natural surveillance (by placing physical features, activities, and people to maximize visibility); natural access control (through the judicial placement of entrances, exits, fencing, landscaping, and lighting); and territorial reinforcement (using buildings, fences, pavement, signs, and landscaping to express ownership).

Critical assets: those assets essential to the minimum operations of the organization, and to ensure the health and safety of the general public.

Damage assessment: the process used to appraise or determine the number of injuries and deaths, damage to public and private property, and the status of key facilities and services.

Design constraint: anything that restricts the design options for a protective system or that creates additional problems for which the design must compensate.

Design opportunity: anything that enhances protection, reduces requirements for protective measures, or solves a design problem.

Detection measure: protective measures that detect intruders, weapons, or explosives; assist in assessing the validity of detection; control access to protected areas; and communicate the appropriate information to the response force. Detection measures include detection systems, assessment systems, and access control system elements.

Detection system elements: Detection measures that detect the presence of intruders, weapons, or explosives. Detection system elements include intrusion detection systems, weapons and explosives detectors, and guards.

Disaster recovery: the process of restoring operations after an interruption in service, including equipment repair/replacement, file recovery/restoration, and resumption of service to users.

Effective stand-off distance: a stand-off distance at which the required level of protection can be shown to be achieved through analysis or can be achieved through building hardening or other mitigating construction or retrofit.

Electronic entry control system: data transmission media, and alarm reporting systems for monitoring, control, and display of various alarm and system information.

Electronic security system (ESS): an integrated system that encompasses interior and exterior sensors, closed circuit television systems for assessment of alarm conditions.

Emergency Alert System (EAS): a communications system of broadcast stations and interconnecting facilities authorized by the Federal Communications Commission (FCC). The system provides the president and other national, state, and local officials the means to broadcast emergency information to the public before, during, and after disasters.

Emergency planning zones (EPZ): areas around a facility for which planning is needed to ensure that prompt and effective actions are taken to protect the health and safety of the public if an accident or disaster occurs.

Entry control point: a continuously or intermittently manned station at which entry to sensitive or restricted areas is controlled.

Entry control station: entry control stations should be provided at main perimeter entrances where security personnel are present. Entry control stations should be located as close as practical to the perimeter entrance to permit personnel inside the station to maintain constant surveillance over the entrance and its approaches.

Equipment closet: a room in which field control equipment such as data gathering panels and power supplies are typically located.

Exclusion area: a restricted area containing a security interest. Uncontrolled movement permits direct access to the item. See also controlled area and limited area.

Explosives disposal container: a small container into which small quantities of explosives may be placed to contain their blast pressures and fragments if the explosive detonates.

Facial recognition: a biometric technology that is based on features of the human face.

Fence protection: an intrusion detection technology that detects a person crossing a fence by various methods such as climbing, crawling, cutting, etc.

Fence sensor: an exterior intrusion detection sensor that detects aggressors as they attempt to climb over, cut through, or otherwise disturb a fence.

Field of view: the visible area in a video picture.

Forced entry: entry to a denied area achieved through force to create an opening in fence, walls, doors, etc., or to overpower guards.

Gamma ray: a high-energy photon emitted from the nucleus of atoms; similar to an x-ray. It can penetrate deeply into body tissue and many materials. Cobalt-60 and Cesium-137 are both strong gamma emitters. Shielding against gamma radiation requires thick layers of dense materials such as lead. Gamma rays are potentially lethal to humans.

Glass-break detector: an intrusion detection sensor that is designed to detect breaking glass either through vibration or acoustics.

Glazing: a material installed in a sash, ventilator, or pane, including glass, plastic, or material such as thin granite installed in a curtain wall.

Hazard mitigation: any action taken to reduce or eliminate the long-term risk to human life and property from hazards. The term is sometimes used in a stricter sense to mean cost-effective measures to reduce the potential for damage to a facility or facilities from a disaster event.

Hazardous material (HAZMAT): any substance or material that, when involved in an accident and released in sufficient quantities, poses a risk to people's health, safety, and/or property. These substances and materials include explosives, radioactive materials, flammable liquids or solids, combustible liquids or solids, poisons, oxidizers, toxins, and corrosive materials.

Incapacitating agents: agents that produce temporary physiological and/or mental effects via action on the central nervous system. Effects may persist for hours or days, but victims usually do not require medical treatment; however, such treatment speeds recovery.

Incident: an occurrence that has been assessed as having an adverse effect on the security or performance of an organization.

Industrial agents: chemicals developed or manufactured for use in industrial operations or research by industry, government, or academia. These chemicals are not primarily manufactured for the specific purpose of producing human casualties or rendering equipment, facilities, or areas dangerous for use.

Insider compromise: a person with authorized access to a facility (an insider) compromises assets by taking advantage of that accessibility.

Intrusion detection sensor: a device that initiates alarm signals by sensing the stimulus, change, or condition for which it was designed.

Intrusion: attacks or attempted attacks from outside the security perimeter of an organization.

Layers of protection: a traditional approach in security engineering using concentric circles extending out from an area to be protected as demarcation points for different security strategies.

Level of protection (LOP): the degree to which an asset is protected against injury or damage from an attack.

Line of sight (LOS): direct observation between two points with the naked eye or hand-held optics.

Man-trap: an access control strategy that uses a pair of interlocking doors to prevent tailgating. Only one door can be unlocked at a time.

Natural protective barriers: natural protective barriers are mountains and deserts, cliffs and ditches, water obstacles, or other terrain features that are difficult to traverse.

Organization integrity: optimal functioning of an organization, free from unauthorized impairment or manipulation.

Organizational areas of control: controls consist of the policies, procedures, practices, and organization structures designed to provide reasonable assurance that business objectives will be achieved and that undesired events will be prevented or detected and corrected.

Perimeter barrier: a fence, wall, vehicle barrier, landform, or line of vegetation applied along an exterior perimeter used to obscure vision, hinder personnel access, or hinder or prevent vehicle access.

Physical security: the part of security concerned with measures/concepts designed to safeguard personnel; to prevent unauthorized access to equipment, installations, materiel, and documents; and to safeguard them against espionage, sabotage, damage, and theft.

Probability of detection (POD): a measure of an intrusion detection sensor's performance in detecting an intruder within its detection zone.

Probability of intercept: the probability that an act of aggression will be detected and that a response force will intercept the aggressor before the asset can be compromised.

Radiological dispersal device (RDD): a device other than a nuclear explosive device designed to disseminate radioactive material to cause destruction, damage, or injury by means of the radiation produced by the decay of such material.

Remote access: use of a modem and communications software to connect to a computer network from a distant location via a telephone line or wireless connection.

Risk management: the identification, assessment, and mitigation of probabilistic security events (risks) in information systems to a level commensurate with the value of the assets protected.

Risk-based management: risk management that considers unquantifiable, speculative events as well as probabilistic events (that is, uncertainty as well as risk).

Safe haven: secure areas within the interior of the facility. A safe haven should be designed such that it requires more time to penetrate by aggressors than it takes for the response force to reach the protected area to rescue the occupants. It may be a haven from a physical attack or air-isolated haven from CBR contamination.

Security engineering: the process of identifying practical, risk-managed short- and long-term solutions to reduce and/or mitigate dynamic man-made hazards by integrating multiple factors, including construction, equipment, manpower, and procedures.

Security plan: a formal document listing the tasks necessary to meet security requirements, a schedule for their accomplishment, and to whom responsibilities for each task are assigned.

Sensitive information: unclassified information, the loss, misuse, or unauthorized disclosure or modification of which could adversely affect the interest of an organization.

Superstructure: the supporting elements of a building above the foundation.

Threat: any circumstance or event that could harm a critical asset through unauthorized access, compromise of data integrity, disruption of service, or physical destruction or impairment.

Toxicity: a measure of the harmful effects produced by a given amount of a toxin on a living organism.

Video motion detection: motion detection technology that looks for changes in the pixels of a video image.

Visual surveillance: the aggressor uses ocular and photographic devices (such as binoculars and cameras with telephoto lenses) to monitor facility or installation operations or to see assets.

Voice recognition: a biometric technology that is based on nuances of the human voice.

Vulnerability assessment: An examination of the ability of a system's current security procedures and controls to withstand assault.

Vulnerability: a flaw in security procedures, software, internal system controls, or implementation of a system of any type that may affect the integrity, confidentiality, accountability, and/or availability of data or services.

Acronyms

AARE	after action report
ACL	access control list
ACP	access control point
ACS	access control system
AECS	automated entry control system
AMS	aerial measuring system
ANS	alert and notification system
ANSI	American National Standards Institute
AOR	area of responsibility
ARAC	atmospheric release advisory capability
BCC	backup control center
BCP	business continuity plan
BDC	bomb data center
BLASTOP	blast-resistant window program
BMS	balanced magnetic switch
BW	biological warfare
CBR	chemical, biological, or radiological
CBRNE	chemical, biological, radiological, nuclear, or explosive
CCTV	closed circuit television
CDC	Centers for Disease Control and Prevention
CDR	call detail report
CDRG	catastrophic disaster response group
CFR	Code of Federal Regulations
CIP	critical infrastructure protection
CIRG	crisis incident response group
CM	consequence management
CMU	concrete masonry unit
CONEX	container express
CONOPS	concept of operations

COR	class of restriction
COS	class of service
CPG	Civil Preparedness Guide
CPTED	crime prevention through environmental design
CPX	command post exercise
CRU	crisis response unit
CT	counterterrorism
CW/CBD	chemical warfare/contraband detection
DBT	design basis threat
DES	data encryption standard
DEST	domestic emergency support team
DFO	disaster field office
DHS	Department of Homeland Security
DMAT	disaster medical assistance team
DMCR	disaster management central resource
DMORT	disaster mortuary operational response team
DoD	Department of Defense
DOE	Department of Energy
DOJ	Department of Justice
DOS	Department of State
DOT	Department of Transportation
DPP	Domestic Preparedness Program
DRC	disaster recovery center
EAS	Emergency Alert System
ECL	emergency classification level
EECS	electronic entry control system
EFR	emergency first responder
EM	emergency management
EMAC	Emergency Medical Assistance Compact
EMI	Emergency Management Institute

EMS	emergency medical services
EOC	emergency operations center
EOD	explosive ordnance disposal
EOP	emergency operating plan
EPA	Environmental Protection Agency
EPCRA	Emergency Planning and Community Right-to-Know Act
EPG	Emergency Planning Guide
EPI	emergency public information
EPZ	emergency planning zone
ERP	emergency response plan
ERT	emergency response team
ERT-A	emergency response team advance element
ERT-N	emergency response team national
ERTU	evidence response team unit
ESC	expandable shelter container
ESF	emergency support function
ESS E	electronic security system
EST	emergency support team
FAsT	field assessment team
FEMA	Federal Emergency Management Agency
FEST	foreign emergency support team
FHBM	flood hazard boundary map
FIA	Federal Insurance Administration
FIPS	Federal Information Processing Standard
FIRM	flood insurance rate map
FIS	flood insurance study
FISCAM	Federal Information Systems Control Audit Manual
FMFIA	Federal Manager's Financial Integrity Act
FOIA	Freedom of Information Act
FOUO	for official use only

FPEIS	final programmatic environmental impact statement
FRERP	Federal Radiological Emergency Response Plan
FRL	facility restriction level
FTX	functional training exercise
GAO	General Accounting Office
GAR	governor's authorized representative
GSA	General Services Administration
HazMat	hazardous material
HHS	Department of Health and Human Services
HIRA	hazard identification and risk assessment
HMRU	hazardous materials response unit
HVAC	heating, ventilation, and air conditioning
IC	incident commander
ICDDC	Interstate Civil Defense and Disaster Compact
ICP	incident command post
ICS	incident command system
IDS	intrusion detection system
IED	improvised explosive device
IEMS	integrated emergency management system
IID	improvised incendiary device
IND	improvised nuclear device
ISO	International Organization for Standardization
JTTF	Joint Terrorism Task Force
JTWG	Joint Terrorism Working Group
LCM	life-cycle management
LEPC	local emergency planning committee
LOS	line of sight
MEP	mission essential process
MOU/A	memorandum of understanding/agreement
MPOP	minimum points of presence

NBC	nuclear, biological, and chemical
NDA	National Defense Area
NDMS	National Disaster Medical System
NDPO	National Domestic Preparedness Office
NEST	Nuclear Emergency Search Team
NETC	National Emergency Training Center
NFA	National Fire Academy
NFIP	National Flood Insurance Program
NFPC	National Fire Protection Code
NIOSH	National Institute for Occupational Safety and Health
NMRT	National Medical Response Team
NRC	Nuclear Regulatory Commission
NRT	National Response Team
NSC	National Security Council
NTIS	National Technical Information Service
ODP	Office of Disaster Preparedness
OEP	Office of Emergency Preparedness
OES	Office of Emergency Services
OFCM	Office of the Federal Coordinator for Meteorology
OMB	Office of Management and Budget
OSHA	Occupational Safety and Health Administration
PAZ	protective action zone
PCC	Policy Coordinating Committee
PCCIP	President's Commission on Critical Infrastructure Protection
PL	Public Law
POC	point of contact
POD	probability of detection
POI	probability of intrusion
POV	privately owned vehicle
RACES	Radio Amateur Civil Emergency Service

RAP	Radiological Assistance Program
RCRA	Research Conservation and Recovery Act
RDD R	radiological dispersal device
RDT&E	research, development, test, and evaluation
REACT	radio emergency associated communications team
REAC/TS	radiation emergency assistance center/training site
ROC	regional operations center
ROD	record of decision
RRP	regional response plan
RRT	regional response team
SAA	state administrative agency
SAC	special agent in charge (FBI)
SCC	security control center
SCO	state coordinating officer
SEB	state emergency board
SEL	standardized equipment list
SEMA	state emergency management agency
SERC	state emergency response commission
SLA	service level agreement
SLG	state and local guide
SNM	special nuclear material
SOP	standard operating procedure
SSS	small shelter system
TEA T	threat environment assessment
TERC	Tribal Emergency Response Commission
TIA	Terrorist Incident Appendix
TIM	toxic industrial material
UC	unified command
UCS	unified command system
UFAS	uniform federal accessibility standards

UFC	unified facilities criteria
USC	U.S. Code
USDA	U.S. Department of Agriculture
USFA	U.S. Fire Administration
USGBC	U.S. Green Building Council
USGS	U.S. Geological Survey
US&R	urban search and rescue
VAP	vulnerability assessment plan
WINGARD	window glazing analysis response and design
WINLAC	window light analysis code
WMD	weapons of mass destruction

C

Action Step Checklists

There are several steps that organizations can take to help improve the physical security of IT assets. Recommended steps are included at the end of each chapter. The action steps listed in this appendix are in the same order as they appear in the chapters of the book. The step numbers also match the step numbers as they are presented in the chapters; step number 1.01, for example, is from Chapter 1.

Action Steps for Evaluating Security Threats

Step Number	Action Step
1.01	Establish a working group to evaluate how the organization is addressing the physical security of IT assets.
1.02	Select members of the working group from IT, human resources, legal, and other departments.
1.03	Designate two co-chairs for the working group.
1.04	Convene the working group to discuss how they can best organize themselves to address physical security of IT assets.
1.05	The working group should set a timeline for activities based on the action steps contained in subsequent chapters of this book.
1.06	The working group should create subgroups to examine the practices included in this chapter to determine their applicability to your organization.
1.07	Once the subgroups have determined applicability of practices in this chapter, plans should be formulated for implementation or, when necessary, further study should be conducted as stated in the practices.
1.08	Timelines should be established for the studies and adequate time should be allowed for the studies to be conducted. Upon completion, the study groups should report back to the main working group.

Action Steps for Evaluating Security Threats (continued)

Step Number	Action Step
1.09	The working group should evaluate the results of any studies conducted and formulate recommendations to management for appropriate changes to existing procedures or the implementation of new procedures.
1.10	When appropriate, the working group should formulate or at least comment on the budgets for building renovations that can help to improve physical security.
1.11	Preserve the research and evaluations done at this phase for use when developing a comprehensive physical IT security plan as discussed in later chapters.

Action Steps for Establishing a Physical IT Security Function

Step Number	Action Step
2.01	Evaluate how responsibilities for physical IT security can be assigned to staff and distributed among various departments.
2.02	Evaluate how economic responsibilities for physical IT security can be distributed among various departments.
2.03	Evaluate the role that corporate security can perform in the development and support of a physical IT security effort.
2.04	Evaluate the role that IT security can perform in the development and support of a physical IT security effort.
2.05	Evaluate the role that network security can perform in the development and support of a physical IT security effort.
2.06	Evaluate existing procedures for working with law enforcement by comparing those procedures to the practices discussed in this chapter. Prepare recommendations to management on how procedures should be modified or what new procedures should be implemented.
2.07	Evaluate the need for security guards, officers, and consultants. Prepare an analysis for management on how these services may be useful to your organization.

Action Steps for Establishing a Physical IT Security Function (continued)

Step Number	Action Step
2.08	Evaluate internal reporting and alert systems by comparing procedures to the practices discussed in this chapter. Prepare recommendations to management on how procedures should be modified or what new procedures should be implemented.
2.09	The working group should convene and review the evaluations recommended in the preceding action steps and make recommendations to management for implementation.

Action Steps for Organizing to Develop a Physical IT Security PlanStep

Step Number	Action Step
3.01	Finalize the decision about how responsibilities for physical IT security will be distributed across departments.
3.02	Finalize, or at least solidify, the decision about how economic responsibilities for physical IT security will be distributed across departments.
3.03	Assign new members to the physical IT security working group from all of the departments that will have some responsibility for implementing the new physical IT security plan.
3.04	Convene the working group and designate two co-chairs to lead the reconstituted physical IT security working group.
3.05	Evaluate the organization's various risk exposure analyses to determine their usefulness in the planning process as well as any goals or standards that physical security planning should meet in order to mitigate the risks that an organization faces.
3.06	Evaluate insurance policies to ensure that your physical IT security practices are consistent with minimum requirements set in insurance policies.
3.07	Evaluate insurance policies to determine if there are physical IT security practices that can result in discounts on premiums to reduce insurance costs.

Action Steps for Organizing to Develop a Physical IT Security Plan (continued)

Step Number	Action Step
3.08	Evaluate laws and regulations that may require general or specific physical IT security practices with which you may need to comply.
3.09	Assemble all of these evaluations and prepare to move on to the next phase of physical IT security planning and procedure development.

Action Steps for Assembling Needed Information to Develop a Physical IT Security Plan

Step Number	Action Step
4.01	Identify which areas (from those listed in this chapter) need to have physical IT security policies and procedures developed for them.
4.02	Develop a tentative list of procedures that need to be developed for each of the areas you identified as needing physical security procedures.
4.03	Review the practices in Chapter 1 that are recommended to counter various types of threats and select those that best meet the needs of your organization.
4.04	Assign members of the working group the responsibility for drafting procedures for those areas that you have determined need procedures.
4.05	Convene the physical IT working group and review the status of work on developing the tentative list of needed procedures and prepare to move ahead with developing draft procedures.

Action Steps for Developing and Documenting Methods and Procedures

Step Number	Action Step
5.01	Assemble the checklists from Chapter 4 that show what physical IT security procedures should cover for each area and the list of procedures that the working group decided should be developed. Use those lists to prioritize procedure development.
5.02	Devise a uniform format for documenting procedures.

Action Steps for Developing and Documenting Methods and Procedures (continued)

Step Number	Action Step
5.03	Draft and test needed procedures.
5.04	Finalize the procedures and create documentation.
5.05	Use the list of procedures that the working group decided were necessary procedures and check that they have been developed and are included in the documentation.

Action Steps for Auditing and Testing Security Procedures

Step Number	Action Step
6.01	Develop a set of checklists to audit physical IT security procedures.
6.02	Devise a test process to test related physical IT security procedures such as an emergency evacuation of the data center.
6.03	Establish a tentative schedule for audits and tests of physical IT security procedures.
6.04	Develop an embedded monitoring and security violation reporting process for your organization.
6.05	Assign a subgroup of the physical IT working group to develop appropriate methods to audit and test compliance with procedures in a data center.
6.06	Assign a subgroup of the physical IT working group to develop appropriate methods to test adherence to security procedures for wiring and cabling.
6.07	Assign a subgroup of the physical IT working group to develop appropriate methods to test adherence to security procedures for remote computing.
6.08	Assign a subgroup of the physical IT working group to develop appropriate methods to test adherence to security procedures for desktop computers.
6.09	Assign a subgroup of the physical IT working group to develop appropriate methods to test adherence to security procedures for department-based servers.

Action Steps for Auditing and Testing Security Procedures (continued)

Step Number	Action Step
6.10	Assign a subgroup of the physical IT working group to develop appropriate methods to test adherence to security procedures for telecom and datacom equipment.
6.11	Assign a subgroup of the physical IT working group to develop appropriate methods to test adherence to security procedures for manufacturing control equipment.
6.12	Assign a subgroup of the physical IT working group to develop appropriate methods to test adherence to security procedures for surveillance and alarm systems.
6.13	Convene the working group and review the methods developed by the subgroups for their assigned areas.
6.14	Conduct a test of all of the checklists the subgroups devised for auditing compliance with security procedures in their assigned areas.
6.15	Based on the experience of the working group, revise the checklist for auditing compliance with physical IT security procedures.
6.16	Assign a subgroup to devise a security violation reporting form and procedure.
6.17	Convene the working group to review the security violation reporting form and develop a recommendation to management for the adoption of the form and the reporting procedure.

Action Steps for Establishing an Incident Response Team

Step Number	Action Step
7.01	Assign a subgroup of the physical IT security working group to evaluate existing incident response procedures in your organization to determine if they meet the needs of responding to a physical IT security incident.
7.02	Assign a subgroup of the physical IT security working group to recommend amendments to your existing incident response procedures or develop new procedures for response.
7.03	Select the members of your incident response team from those departments that have various responsibilities for physical IT security (as was recommended in Chapter 4).

Action Steps for Establishing an Incident Response Team (continued)

Step Number	Action Step
7.04	Have the members of the incident response team designate an alternate from their department to serve as a team member in their absence.
7.05	Convene the members of the incident response team and their alternates to review the response procedures.
7.06	Review the first report, confirmation, and mobilization procedures to determine if they are adequate in scope to mobilize a response to an incident.
7.07	Review the process to notify management, alert departments, and inform end-users to determine if they are adequate in scope to support a response to an incident.
7.08	Review the procedures for preserving evidence of a crime to determine if they are adequate in scope to meet the needs of reporting a crime to law enforcement agencies.
7.09	Review the procedures for notifying law enforcement that a computer crime has occurred to determine if they are adequate in scope to meet the needs of the organization.
7.10	Review the processes of analyzing and acting on lessons learned from an incident to determine if they can help the organization improve response.
7.11	Hold a tabletop simulation of an incident and have the members of the response team describe what they would do to respond. Walk through the incident step by step as described in this chapter.
7.12	Review the results of the tabletop simulation of an incident and have the members recommend changes to the incident response plan, if necessary.
7.13	Evaluate the role that the incident response team should play in planning for or responding to a natural disaster or a deliberate damaging incident and develop appropriate procedures.

Action Steps Training Program for Organization Staff

Step Number	Action Step
8.01	Evaluate the training needs for your IT and security professionals and recommend training programs and certification levels appropriate for your organization.
8.02	Establish a subgroup of the physical IT security working group to lead an effort to develop an organizationwide training program.
8.03	Establish a project schedule for the development and testing of the training material.
8.04	Develop a basic awareness training program that can be used as an introduction to an in-depth physical security training program or as a module in other training efforts, and also develop a stand alone seminar that can used to promote awareness.
8.05	Develop and test all of your training modules and make modifications based on evaluator input.
8.06	Designate an HR staff person to coordinate the record keeping process for employees who have participated in the training.
8.07	Initiate the training process.
8.08	After several training sessions have taken place, evaluate the response to the training and determine if any changes should be made to the material or the process.

Action Steps to Take for the Future of Physical Security for IT Assets

Step Number	Action Step
9.01	Evaluate the impact of national security strategies on your operations and security plans. Make recommendations to management on how you can maximize the benefit you receive from those plans.
9.02	Evaluate the potential benefit of becoming a member of one or more of the ISACs. Make recommendations to management on how you can maximize the benefit you receive from those organizations.
9.03	Evaluate ways in which you can monitor the activities of government agencies such as DHS to determine if new activities or information from the agencies can help you improve your physical IT security. Make recommendations to management on how you can maximize the benefit you receive from monitoring those agencies.

Physical Security Planning Checklists

There are several checklists and sample forms contained in the chapters of this book. For your convenience they have all been assembled in this appendix. The original table or form number is included in parentheses after the title of each exhibit.

Practices to Reduce Attacks by Employees (Table 1.3)

Notify security staff when an employee has been terminated or suspended.
When you do not have a security staff, notify all managers and supervisors when an employee has been terminated or suspended.
Maintain strict policies on access to facilities by nonemployees and train all employees on those policies.
If terminated or suspended employees had been issued keys, ensure that keys are returned.
Change the locks for which any angry former employee had keys.
Change key codes to electronic doors immediately after an employee has been terminated or suspended.
Disable user rights for computers or communications systems held by the former or suspended employee.

Practices to Reduce Attacks by Activists (Table 1.4)

Notify security staff of the activist groups that may have targeted your organization or similar organizations.
When you do not have a security staff, notify all managers and supervisors of the activist groups that may have targeted your organization or similar organizations.
Ensure that the primary services for the building are secured, including electricity, telecommunications, gas, water, and sewer, in a manner that makes it difficult to access and harm control systems and connections.
Develop contingency plans for disruptions in primary services.
Determine if critical or sensitive information is stored or handled at the building and develop contingency plans and recovery plans for operations.
Identify and secure locations of important and expensive equipment.
Minimize the circulation of information about what activities take place in a facility to the general public.
Minimize the profile of activities that take place in a facility by limiting the identification of the facility in scientific papers, press releases, or public mention by researchers or executives about the facility.
If possible, draw attention to other facilities owned by the organization and use those facilities as decoys for activist actions.

Practices to Reduce Attacks by Vandals (Table 1.5)

Notify security staff of recent or ongoing vandal activity in areas around a facility.
When you do not have a security staff, notify all managers and supervisors of recent or ongoing vandal activity in areas around a facility.
Maintain basic building security functions such as night lighting, closed circuit cameras to monitor activities, and intrusion detection systems that activate alarms to initiate response by private security forces or local police.
Post signs warning of no trespassing and awards for information leading to the arrest of individuals who damage property.
Work with local law enforcement agencies to support community watch programs and other crime reduction efforts.

Practices to Reduce Attacks by Saboteurs (Table 1.6)

Notify security staff of any known saboteurs who may be targeting your organization.
When you do not have a security staff, notify all managers and supervisors of any known saboteurs who may be targeting your organization.
If a threat of sabotage is detected, hire private investigators to help determine who may be supporting such efforts.
If specific intelligence is gathered about supporting organizations or specific individuals, consider notifying the FBI or other appropriate law enforcement agency.
If specific threats or extortion schemes are detected, consider notifying the FBI or other appropriate law enforcement agency.
As is helpful with dealing with other possible intruders or attackers, the internal layout of a building or facility should not be clearly labeled. (For example, do not post signs on doors to identify things like telecommunications closets, server rooms, or data processing centers.)
Use key code or other locks to secure areas such as server rooms, telecommunications closets, or data processing centers.
Use surveillance cameras in areas such as server rooms, telecommunications closets, or data processing centers that can record and store images of activities in those areas.

Practices to Reduce Attacks by Thieves and Spies (Table 1.7)

Notify security staff of known thieves or spies who may have targeted your organization.
When you do not have a security staff, notify all managers and supervisors about known thieves or spies who may have targeted your organization.
Discuss specific knowledge about known thieves or spies who may have targeted your organization with the FBI or other appropriate law enforcement organization.
Thieves or spies often use social engineering methods to infiltrate or obtain information about an organization, and employees should be trained to not provide information to outsiders.

Practices to Reduce Attacks by Thieves and Spies (Table 1.7) (continued)

Thieves or spies often use dumpster diving to obtain scraps of information about an organization that can be used in social engineering efforts to obtain further information. This means that you need to be very careful about what you throw in your trash cans and should shred any paper that has any information on it about the organization. Electronic media also should be thoroughly destroyed before disposal.
If computers are left on overnight, users should log off of their systems to reduce ease of access.
Password discipline should be maintained and passwords should be complex and changed frequently.

Practices to Reduce Attacks by Domestic Terrorists (Table 1.8)

Notify security staff of any specific knowledge about potential domestic terrorist attacks.
When you do not have a security staff, notify all managers and supervisors of any specific knowledge about potential domestic terrorist attacks.
Work with local law enforcement agencies to determine if domestic terrorists are a threat to your organization or organizations with nearby facilities.
If your technology is located in a building with other occupants, conduct your own assessment of the attractiveness of those organizations as a target for domestic terrorists. If you conclude that your technology is located in a building occupied by attractive targets, consider moving it to another location.
Conduct your own assessment of the relative location of your facility to the location of attractive targets such as government buildings, iconic properties, major commercial centers, or major transportation centers. If you conclude that your technology is located close to such targets, consider moving it to another location.
Conduct an assessment of vulnerability of your building to terrorist attacks, including how well the building can be secured; structural systems; building envelope; mechanical systems; heating, ventilation, and air conditioning (HVAC); plumbing, gas, and electrical systems; fire alarm and other security systems. The key question to ask is how accessible are these systems to individuals who would like to do damage? If these systems are too open or cannot be secured, consider hiring an architect for redesign or moving your technology to another location.

Practices to Reduce Attacks by Domestic Terrorists (Table 1.8) (continued)

Conduct an assessment of the proximity of your facilities to locations that host events, attractions, festivals, celebrations, open-air markets, parades, rallies, demonstrations, marches, or religious services that could be targets of domestic terrorists. If your technology is in a facility that is close to such locations used by groups that have been targeted by domestic terrorists in the past, you should bolster security or consider moving the technology.
Eliminate potential building access through utility tunnels, corridors, manholes, and storm water runoff culverts.
Evaluate the need for barriers to keep out attackers, including passive barriers such as bollards, walls, hardened fences (steel cable interlaced), trenches, ponds/basins, concrete planters, street furniture, plantings, trees, sculptures, and fountains. Also consider active barriers, including pop-up bollards, swing arm gates, and rotating plates and drums.
Evaluate parking and vehicle access systems to determine how close to your building attackers can move a vehicle under normal operating conditions. If vehicles cannot be kept a reasonable distance, consider redesigning roads and parking lots to keep unauthorized vehicles at least 100 feet away from the building.
Develop and enforce procedures to control internal building parking, underground parking garages, and access to service areas and loading docks.
Minimize opportunities for attackers to conceal packages by keeping landscaping items, hedges, shrubbery, large plants, outdoor furniture, trash receptacles, mailboxes, and newspaper vending machines away from your building.
Ensure that emergency vehicles have access to the building and that fire hydrants are readily accessible if they are needed.
Ensure that critical assets are not near an entrance to the building, including telecommunications equipment, utility closets, and building control systems.
Evaluate the planning and zoning efforts related to future structures that are to be erected near your building. If these efforts will result in increasing the vulnerability of your facility, consider lobbying against the efforts through local political systems.
Develop a suspicious package screening program for deliveries arriving at your facility.
Develop procedures to deal with emergency evacuation and lockdown of equipment in the event of a bomb or chemical or biological threat.

Practices to Reduce Attacks by International Terrorists (Table 1.9)

Notify security staff of known threats from international terrorists.
When you do not have a security staff, notify all managers and supervisors of known threats from international terrorists.
Work with local law enforcement agencies to determine whether international terrorists are a threat to your organization or organizations with nearby facilities.
Conduct your own assessment of your organization profile and how or why you may become a target of international terrorists.
If your technology is located in a building with other occupants, conduct your own assessment of the attractiveness of those organizations as targets for international terrorists. If you conclude that your technology is located in a building occupied by attractive targets, consider moving it to another location.
Conduct your own assessment of the location of your facility in relationship to government buildings, iconic properties, major commercial centers, or major transportation centers that may be attractive targets for international terrorists. If you conclude that your technology is located close to such targets, consider moving it to another location.
If you receive packages or mail from other countries you need to develop a suspicious package screening program for deliveries arriving at your facility from.
If you receive shipments of goods or raw materials from other countries you need to develop a screening program for containers, boxes, or crates arriving at your facility.
Conduct background checks of your foreign suppliers to determine if they have relationships with known terrorist organizations.
Restrict the information about your organization that you provide to foreign suppliers or customers.
Conduct background checks of visitors from foreign suppliers or customers to determine if they have relationships with known terrorist organizations before the individuals are allowed into your facilities.
Establish a monitoring system to determine if your organization is mentioned on the websites or in the communications of terrorist groups or terrorist sympathizers and supporters.

Practices to Reduce Damage from Natural Disasters (Table 1.10)

Evaluate the physical location of a facility to determine if it is vulnerable to flooding. If the facility is vulnerable, then IT equipment must be located in a place from which it can be removed temporarily or in a place that is the least susceptible to flooding.
Evaluate the physical location of IT assets within a facility to determine if it is vulnerable to leakage in the event of heavy rains or melting snow. If the location is vulnerable, then the facility should be reinforced against leakage or the equipment should be moved to another location within the facility or to another facility.
Develop a removal plan for IT assets in the event that a building is damaged to the point at which it cannot be utilized. This includes disconnecting and packing the equipment, transporting the equipment, and storing or reinstalling the equipment at an alternative location.
Develop procedures to shut down equipment and secure facilities in the event that personnel must be evacuated from a facility for an extended period. This should at minimum include disconnecting power and installing protective covering for the equipment.
Establish an offsite backup location to physically protect duplicate media, documentation, and data in the event that the primary location becomes inaccessible or is destroyed.
Integrate these procedures into the emergency response, disaster recovery, and business continuity plans of your organization.

Practices to Reduce Damage from Random Incidents (Table 1.11)

Establish a response plan for your building and IT asset security that can be executed quickly in case of a random incident that threatens a facility or the personnel in that facility.
Establish a notification procedure to inform management that a random incident has disrupted or may disrupt operations.
Establish a notification procedure to inform employees that a random incident has disrupted or may disrupt operations and instruct them as to what actions they should take.
Rehearse all of the random incident procedures and modify procedures if necessary.
Integrate these procedures into the emergency response, disaster recovery, and business continuity plans of your organization.

Departmental Responsibilities for Physical IT Security (Table 2.1)

Department	Physical Security Responsibility
Central IT	Advise on procedures that affect data centers and distributed computing, and advise on security technology
Data Network Management	Advise on procedures that affect networking equipment, cabling, WAN connections, and remote computing
Telecommunications	Advise on procedures that affect telecom equipment, voice terminals, and carrier connections
Organization Security	Implement access control procedures, and advise on physical security for equipment and facilities
Buildings and grounds	Install locks, security devices, and access control systems, and maintain security systems
Purchasing	Acquire needed equipment and security systems
Legal	Advise on policies and forms that employees sign regarding adherence to policies
Human Resources	Manage training programs and retain signed policy statements of employees
PR and Internal Communications	Promote physical IT security awareness
Manufacturing, Business Operations, and Other Functional or Product-Focused Departments	Assist in implementing physical IT security plans and procedures

Financial Responsibilities for Physical IT Security (Table 2.2)

Department	Financial Responsibility
Central IT	Costs of securing data centers, centralized servers, staff time for advising other departments on security procedures
Data Network Management	Costs of securing networking equipment, cabling, and WAN connections
Telecommunications	Costs of securing centralized telecom equipment and carrier connections

Financial Responsibilities for Physical IT Security (Table 2.2) (continued)

Department	Financial Responsibility
Organization Security	Staff time to implement access control procedures and advise on physical security for equipment and facilities
Buildings and grounds	Costs of locks, security devices, and access control systems and the costs to install and maintain security systems
Purchasing	Staff time to acquire needed equipment and security systems
Legal	Staff time to advise on policies and forms that employees sign regarding adherence to policies
Human Resources	Staff time to manage training programs and retain signed policy statements of employees
PR and Internal Communications	Staff time and costs of materials to promote physical IT security awareness
Manufacturing, Business Operations, and Other Functional or Product-Focused Departments	Costs of equipment to secure user terminals, desktop computers, peripherals, and voice equipment used in the department and remote computing devices used by employees

Elements Required for Plan Completion (Table 4.1)

Element	Status (completed, pending, not applicable)
Departmental responsibilities for plan elements or implementing procedures (Chapter 2)	Enter status for each area in this column.
Reviews of applicable practices included in chapter 1	
Detailed evaluation of the role corporate security can perform to support physical IT security efforts (Chapter 2).	
Detailed evaluation of the role that IT security can perform to support of a physical IT security efforts (Chapter 2)	
Detailed evaluation of the role network security can perform to support physical IT security efforts (Chapter 2)	

Elements Required for Plan Completion (Table 4.1) (continued)

Element	Status (completed, pending, not applicable)
Detailed evaluation of existing procedures for working with law enforcement (Chapter 2)	
Detailed evaluation of the need for security guards, officers, and consultants (Chapter 2)	
Detailed evaluation of internal reporting and alert systems (Chapter 2)	
Detailed evaluations of various risk exposure analyses, including the cyber security plan, disaster recovery plan, and business continuity plan that indicate what must be done to align the physical IT security plan with other risk mitigation efforts (Chapter 3)	
Evaluations of insurance policy requirements and opportunities for discounts in premiums by implementing specific physical IT security practices (Chapter 3)	
Evaluations of laws and regulations that may require general or specific physical IT security practices with which you may need to comply (Chapter 3)	

Checklist for Data Center Security Procedures (Table 4.3)

Types of Procedures Needed	Status (completed, pending, not applicable)
If the data center occupies the entire building, then the plan needs to address security for the exterior of the building, lobby areas, utility areas, loading docks, offices, and each subarea of the rooms in which there is IT equipment.	Enter status for each area in this column.
If the data center occupies only part of a building, then the plan needs to address security for IT staff offices and each subarea of the rooms in which there is IT equipment.	

Checklist for Data Center Security Procedures (Table 4.3) (continued)

Types of Procedures Needed	Status (completed, pending, not applicable)
Access control and access management are key elements of a data center security plan and should indicate who has access, how access is granted, how visitors and vendors are managed, and how to deal with breaches of access policies.	
How and when should a lead security officer or manager regularly review access reports?	
What are the procedures for securing selected equipment, cabling systems, encryption equipment, media rooms, and storage cabinets or areas that contain the most sensitive types of information?	
Note security for utility systems, including air-conditioning, power supplies, network connections, and emergency power systems.	
List security procedures for business-hour operations, after-hour operations, and emergency operations.	
How are up-to-date logs maintained of all equipment, which includes serial numbers and configuration information?	
How are up-to-date lists of personnel authorized to access sensitive areas managed?	
How are environmental settings in equipment rooms maintained?	
How are incoming and outgoing equipment, documents, and supplies signed in and out?	
How and where are incoming packages inspected and opened before contents are brought into the data center?	
How and where are fire suppression systems installed?	
What type of protective containers should be used for sensitive material, including fire-resistant or burglar-resistant standards?	
How are printed materials and used magnetic media disposed of and who is responsible for the disposal?	
If closed-circuit monitors are used, procedures are needed for their use and maintenance.	

Checklist for Wiring and Cabling Security Procedures (Table 4.4)

Types of Procedures Needed	Status (completed, pending, not applicable)
How is access to wiring and cabling areas controlled and monitored?	Enter status for each area in this column.
What types of doors and locks are used to secure wiring and cabling areas?	
What types of alarms or monitoring systems are used for controlling access to wiring and cabling areas?	
Who can authorize access to wiring and cabling areas?	
How are service providers monitored when and if they need to access wiring and cabling areas?	
How are maintenance and access logs for wiring and cabling areas maintained?	
How are keys or key codes for the wiring and cabling areas managed and controlled?	
How are the signals transmitted over wiring and cabling protected from interception?	

Checklist for Remote and Mobile Device Security Procedures (Table 4.5)

Types of Procedures Needed	Status (completed, pending, not applicable)
How are users automatically logged off the host system when it is not being used?	Enter status for each area in this column.
How are user profiles and passwords managed on remote computing devices?	
Note environmental and structural protection for remote computing devices.	
Note physical access controls for remote and mobile computing devices.	
Include property tags and other identification systems for mobile computing devices.	
How is used equipment is disposed of and who is responsible for disposal	

Checklist for Desktop Computing Devices Security Procedures (Table 4.6)

Types of Procedures Needed	Status (completed, pending, not applicable)
Secure placement and protection of equipment within offices or other work areas.	Enter status for each area in this column.
Provide protection for cabling, plugs, and other wires that connect the devices to your network.	
How are users automatically logged off the host system when it is not being used?	
List environmental and structural protection for desktop computing devices.	
Include property tags and other identification systems for desktop computing devices.	
Note security for computer cases to deter unauthorized entry into systems as well as removal or installation of items such as memory, boards, ports, etc.	
List theft deterrent procedures, which may include lockdown.	
How are desktop computers protected from electrical surges or power outages?	
How is used equipment disposed of and who is responsible for disposal?	

Checklist for Department-Based Servers Security Procedures (Table 4.7)

Types of Procedures Needed	Status (completed, pending, not applicable)
How are server areas protected in offices or other work areas?	Enter status for each area in this column.
Provide protection for cabling, plugs, and other wires that connect the devices to your network or connect the servers to local devices.	
Use property tags and other identification systems for department-based servers.	

Checklist for Department-Based Servers Security Procedures (Table 4.7) (continued)

Types of Procedures Needed	Status (completed, pending, not applicable)
Provide security for department-based server cases to deter unauthorized entry into systems as well as removal or installation of items such as memory, boards, ports, etc.	
List theft deterrent procedures, which may include lockdown or enclosure security.	
How are department-based servers protected from electrical surges or power outages?	
How is used equipment disposed of and who is responsible for disposal?	

Checklist for Telecom and Datacom Equipment Security Procedures (Table 4.8)

Types of Procedures Needed	Status (completed, pending, not applicable)
Provide secure placement and protection of equipment within offices, other work areas, wiring and cabling areas, and in the data center.	Enter status for each area in this column.
Use property tags and other identification systems for telecom and datacom equipment.	
List types of doors and locks used to secure telecom and datacom equipment areas as well as the types of racks or mounting devices that should be used to install the equipment.	
What types of alarms or monitoring systems are used for controlling access to telecom and datacom equipment?	
Who can authorize access to telecom and datacom equipment areas?	
How are service providers monitored when and if they need to access telecom and datacom equipment areas?	
How are maintenance and access for telecom and datacom equipment maintained?	

Checklist for Telecom and Datacom Equipment Security Procedures (Table 4.8) (continued)

Types of Procedures Needed	Status (completed, pending, not applicable)
How are keys or key codes for telecom and datacom equipment areas managed and controlled?	
How and when are voice system user logs reviewed and how are reports of misuse handled?	
How is used telecom and datacom equipment disposed of and who is responsible for disposal?	

Checklist for Manufacturing Control Equipment Security Procedures (Table 4.9)

Types of Procedures Needed	Status (completed, pending, not applicable)
Provide secure placement and protection of equipment within other work areas, including cabinetry, rack mounting, and relative location to other types of equipment.	Enter status for each area in this column.
Provide protection for cabling, plugs, and other wires that connect the devices to your network or to automated manufacturing equipment.	
Use property tags and other identification systems for manufacturing control equipment.	
List he types of alarms or monitoring systems used for controlling access to manufacturing control equipment.	
How are service providers monitored when and if they need to work on manufacturing control equipment?	
How are maintenance and access logs for manufacturing control equipment maintained?	
How is used manufacturing control equipment disposed of and who is responsible for disposal?	

Checklist for Surveillance and Alarm System Security Procedures (Table 4.10)

Types of Procedures Needed	Status (completed, pending, not applicable)
Provide secure lacement and protection of surveillance and alarm systems within offices, other work areas, lobbies, and exterior areas of the buildings.	Enter status for each area in this column.
Provide protection for cabling, plugs, and other wires that connect the surveillance and alarm systems to your network or to outside networks used to notify emergency service providers.	
Use property tags and other identification systems for surveillance and alarm systems.	
List the types of doors and locks used to secure surveillance and alarm system areas.	
Who can authorize access to surveillance and alarm system areas and how are maintenance and access logs for surveillance and alarm systems maintained?	
How are service providers monitored when and if they need to access surveillance and alarm systems?	
How keys or key codes surveillance and alarm system areas are managed and controlled.	
How is used surveillance and alarm equipment disposed of and who is responsible for disposal?	

Checklist for Material Needed to Start Developing Procedures (Table 5.1)

Types of Procedures Needed	Status (completed, pending, not applicable)
List of procedures needed to support disaster recovery plans	Enter status for each area in this column.
List of procedures needed to support business continuity plans	
List of procedures needed to support cyber security plans	

Checklist for Material Needed to Start Developing Procedures (Table 5.1) (continued)

Types of Procedures Needed	Status (completed, pending, not applicable)
List of procedures needed to be in compliance with laws and regulations	
List of procedures needed to be in compliance with insurance policy requirements	
List of procedures needed to obtain reduced insurance premiums	
List of selected practices from Chapter 1	
List of needed procedures from checklists in Chapter 4	

Sample Procedure Format (Figure 5.1)

Procedure name	Procedure number
Purpose of the procedure	
Responsible departments	
Details of the procedure	
Plans or policies procedure supports	Date of last revision
Page x of x	

Sample Procedure Violation Report (Figure 8.1)

Date	Reporting Employee
Procedure name	Procedure number
Who violated the procedure (if known)	
Reason for the violation (if known)	
Details of the violation	
Training status of the violator (if known)	Date of last revision of the procedure

Index